LYNCHIAN

Also by John Higgs

I Have America Surrounded
The KLF
Stranger Than We Can Imagine
Watling Street
The Future Starts Here
William Blake Now
William Blake vs the World
Love and Let Die
Exterminate/Regenerate

LYNCHIAN

The Spell of David Lynch

John Higgs

WEIDENFELD & NICOLSON

First published in Great Britain in 2025 by Weidenfeld & Nicolson,
an imprint of The Orion Publishing Group Ltd
Carmelite House, 50 Victoria Embankment
London EC4Y 0DZ

An Hachette UK Company

The authorised representative in the EEA is Hachette Ireland,
8 Castlecourt Centre, Dublin 15, D15 XTP3, Ireland (email: info@hbgi.ie)

3 5 7 9 10 8 6 4

Copyright © John Higgs 2025

The moral right of John Higgs to be identified as
the author of this work has been asserted in accordance
with the Copyright, Designs and Patents Act of 1988.

All rights reserved. No part of this publication may be
reproduced, stored in a retrieval system, or transmitted
in any form or by any means, electronic, mechanical,
photocopying, recording, or otherwise, without the
prior permission of both the copyright owner and the
above publisher of this book.

A CIP catalogue record for this book is
available from the British Library.

ISBN (Hardback) 978 1 3996 3731 2
ISBN (Ebook) 978 1 3996 3732 9
ISBN (Audio) 978 1 3996 3733 6

Typeset at The Spartan Press Ltd,
Lymington, Hants

Printed and bound in Great Britain by Clays Ltd,
Elcograf S.p.A.

www.weidenfeldandnicolson.co.uk
www.orionbooks.co.uk

For all at the East Sussex Psychedelic Film Club

'Energy, Peril, Success'

– Motto of Boise, Idaho

I

After David Lynch died in January 2025, a public shrine spontaneously appeared around a bright, cheerful mascot at Bob's Big Boy restaurant in Burbank, California. To the uninitiated, the collection of objects placed there by grieving fans must have seemed strange and unfathomable.

There were many bunches of flowers, some of which had donuts stuffed within. Alongside these were cookies, cups of coffee, cans of creamed corn and packets of Cheetos. There were many loose cigarettes, as well as packets of Marlboro and American Spirit – an unexpected choice, perhaps, to mark the death of someone who died of emphysema. There were numerous photographs of Laura Palmer, a fictional schoolgirl murdered by her own father. Alongside these were many heartfelt letters, drawings of the baby from the film *Eraserhead*, numerous toy owls and at least one log. On the cards that were left, the phrase 'In Heaven, everything is fine' was common, as was the enigmatic statement, 'The owls are not what they seem.' There were also, somehow, several blue roses, wilting and decaying as flowers at shrines do. As Lynch fans know well, the blue rose is a flower that does not exist in nature.

It is not normal for public shrines to appear and mark the death of film directors. When we eventually lose honoured and respected filmmakers like Christopher Nolan or Denis Villeneuve there will be a great deal of sadness, but it seems unlikely that masses of admirers will spontaneously congregate at some public location associated with their lives. Spontaneous public shrines usually only appear after the passing of truly unique people, like David Bowie or Princess Diana. If you feel compelled to behave like this after the death of someone you never met, that person must have affected you very deeply. They must have felt like a significant presence in your life. I suspect that, before he died, few would have expected David Lynch to be honoured in this way – in the early twenty-first century, it was difficult to assess his status in the world of cinema.

From one perspective, Lynch was clearly a huge success. He made ten singular feature films over a period of four decades. His 2001 movie *Mulholland Drive* can be reliably found near the top of lists of the greatest films of the twenty-first century – the LA Film Critics Association called it the best film of the first decade, for example, while a 2016 BBC critics poll voted it the best film of this century and a 2025 *New York Times* poll placed it second. Lynch won the Palme d'Or at Cannes in 1990 for *Wild at Heart* and his 1980 movie *The Elephant Man* was nominated for eight Academy Awards. Over his career, the Academy nominated him three times for the Best Director Oscar, and once for Best Adapted Screenplay. It gave him an Academy Honorary Award in 2019 for 'fearlessly breaking boundaries in pursuit of his singular cinematic vision'. Most film directors can only dream of achievements like these. This is all before you consider his work in television. *Twin Peaks*, the series he created with Mark Frost, is often described as a turning point in television history, the herald that called forth the golden age of television drama in the decades that followed.

Yet at the same time, Lynch was a director who was unable to get a film green-lit for the last nineteen years of his life. The list of his unrealised projects that no one would fund – including *Ronnie Rocket, Dream of the Bovine, Snootworld, Unrecorded Night, One Saliva Bubble* and *Antelope Don't Run No More* – breaks the hearts of Lynch's admirers. The films he did make were usually funded outside of the American studio system, produced either entirely independently like *Eraserhead*, or by European companies such as StudioCanal or the Dino De Laurentiis Corporation. To mainstream Hollywood, Lynch was seen as too strange, too weird and too out of sync with the cinema-going public to risk funding his movies. People went to the cinema to be told stories that satisfied or comforted them, the thinking went. They did not want to pay money to be confused or unsettled. Lynch's films, from this perspective, just didn't make any sense. They were dismissed as art house movies, *avant garde* experiments or pretentious crap. Lynch loved Los Angeles and lived there most of his life, seduced by the light and the city's willingness to dream. Many people in LA loved him back. But the film industry, to its great shame, did not.

After his death, it became abundantly clear just how much David Lynch meant to people. As Naomi Watts said on the American TV show *Live with Kelly and Mark*, 'The outpouring of love – I don't know if you've witnessed it on social media – has been extraordinary because he really affected so many people. Not just the people he worked with, but how he viewed life and what he gave – just such a big heart. So much purity in there.'

The outpouring of affection and grief was striking not just for its size, but for its depth. This was apparent when a selection of Lynch's possessions were auctioned less than six months after his death, and the initial estimates attached to each item proved to be a tiny fraction of what they would eventually fetch. His copies of the script for *Mulholland Drive*, for example, were estimated to sell for $300–500. They ultimately sold for $104,000. His copy of the script for *Ronnie Rocket*, a film he spent many decades trying and failing to get made, was expected to go for less – $200–300. That sold for $195,000. Every single item that was put up for auction, including his books, his tools, his ashtrays, his furniture, his posters and his film memorabilia, massively overshot the estimates and sold for many thousands of dollars. His home espresso machine sold for $45,000, his director's chair made $91,000 and even a single 'Log Lady' mug reached $11,700. The desire to possess something that Lynch had once owned seemed less a question of celebrity memorabilia and more like the recognition of holy relics. It was a sad irony that, if he could have realised these prices for selling the stuff around his house while he was alive, he might have been able to fund one more of his dream movie projects.

People felt close to David Lynch, like he was a friend they had just not met yet. 'There are certain figures that you just feel close to,' the comedian and director Richard Ayoade said as he described his relationship to Lynch's work to podcaster Adam Buxton. 'What they do is so impactful and there seems something very truthful about it, that you have a familiarity.' This sense of connection, ultimately, came from the way that Lynch's films made their audience feel things that other directors' films never could. They showed you previously unimagined depths of your soul and this shocked you into realising that you were larger and richer than you ever thought. For this kindness – for being for ever changed in this way – you could only be immensely grateful.

But how did he do this? What is it about his cinematic bag of tricks – his shots of shadows and flickering electricity, his sinister soundscapes and his heartfelt scores, his dreamlike irrational stories – that affects us so deeply? What, exactly, was David Lynch doing? We don't need to question why we enjoy a film where Tom Cruise hangs from the side of an aeroplane. We understand the appeal of Wes Anderson's mannered, quirky visual compositions, and we're not confused about why the happy ending in a romcom feels so satisfying. But why, exactly, do David Lynch's films affect us like they do? How can he present us with trees swaying in the wind, or a character suddenly becoming another person, or more questions than answers, and it stays with us for ever? And why is it that, when somebody else uses his tricks, it does not achieve the same results?

There is no shortage of unique and extraordinary films, if you are prepared to look for them. There are many wonderful strange, visionary and psychedelic filmmakers at work today – including directors such as Bertrand Mandico, Peter Strickland and Leos Carax. They produce astounding work, often in very challenging conditions. Yet David Lynch remains apart from all these, in a category of one, unique and irreplaceable. What he did was so different and singular that the standard criteria for critiquing films falls apart when confronted by his work. We can take apart his films and list what he was doing, but we struggle to explain what he was doing to *us*, the audience haunted by his films.

The word 'Lynchian' has been used in film circles since 1984. It seems to be a useful, well-understood adjective, and yet, as we will see, no one other than David Lynch has ever been truly Lynchian.

2

The state of Idaho is an immense wilderness of mountains and forests punctuated by tracts of farmland and small towns. Roughly the size of mainland Britain, it is relatively unpopulated, home to only a couple of million people. The towns of Idaho are often a great distance from their nearest neighbour – tiny lights of human settlements in a vast, wild ecosystem where the endless rhythms of the natural world are simultaneously calming and awe-inspiring. In landscapes such as these, people seem small and insignificant.

The natural beauty of Idaho was the backdrop to the formative years of David Keith Lynch, a child born five months after the bombing of Hiroshima and the subsequent ending of the Second World War. Lynch spoke often about the blissful childhood years he spent in Boise, in the American northwest. Boise is the state capital and the largest city in Idaho, but back in the 1950s it still possessed the character of a small town. David was raised in a happy, supportive nuclear family with his mother, father and a younger brother and sister. His father Donald was a research scientist at the Department of Agriculture and his job involved the study of forest ecosystems, so from an early age David was aware that there was more to the trees outside of town than their sturdy, solid appearance suggested. Like the rest of the natural world, they were engaged in a constant dance of growth and decay. 'My father frequently experimented on tree diseases and insects. He had huge forests at his disposal to experiment on,' Lynch told the film writer Chris Rodley. 'I was exposed to insects, disease and growth, in an organic sort of world, like a forest, or even a garden. And this sort of thrills me.'

Young David also knew that as day slips through dusk into night, the natural world transforms. Different systems of predators and prey come into play. Beauty fades with the light and is replaced with something unknowable and difficult to verbalise. Darkness in a landscape such as this can be total, almost suffocatingly so, especially on a cloudy night. It's a type of darkness that people who live in cities never experience, but it was a formative part of David's early years. He recalled being taken out deer hunting at night by his father. 'We drive out of Boise and we're on a two-lane highway. The only light is from the headlights of the car and it's pitch-black. It's hard for people today to imagine this, because there are no roads that are pitch-black.' This image of headlights illuminating the rushing tarmac emerging out of thick, overpowering darkness appears repeatedly throughout Lynch's work, most notably in the openings of *Lost Highway* and *Mulholland Drive*. When you journey out into darkness like this, the only light is that which you bring yourself.

Surrounded by this sea of endless unfathomable darkness and the mysterious process of growth and decay it contained, the lights of home took on a new meaning. Those tiny oases of 1950s American culture – home to televisions, Cadillacs, budding suburbs and Elvis records – were a modern Eden: a seeming paradise of abundance and security bold and bright enough to hold back the eternal sea of darkness that surrounded them. A new way of life, protected, prosperous and privileged with no equal in history, emerged in those post-war years. Technology, ingenuity and marketing kept people in a state of amazement, gratitude and excitement. When he was a child, David's life was usually contained within an area no bigger than a couple of blocks, but that small patch of suburbia was immense in his eyes. It was an entire world, and it contained all that he could ever hope for. You could lose yourself in the lights of that world and never face the darkness outside. 'Because I grew up in a perfect world, other things were a contrast,' Lynch said.

One night in the autumn of the late 1950s, as he was turning from a child into a teenager, David Lynch was playing out in the street with his brother John. It was the Eisenhower years and children were free to roam the neighbourhood as they pleased – even at night. Normally the boys would go in when their father called them, but that hadn't happened this particular night and they were outside later than usual. The streetlights back then were dimmer than modern lights. As Lynch recalled, they made 'night kind of magical because things just go into black'. Nights like these, deep voids of blackness punctuated by islands of thin light, were often silent and still.

'I don't know what we were doing, but from across Shoshone Avenue out of the darkness came kind of like the strangest dream,' Lynch later recalled. As the boys watched, a naked woman, beaten and bleeding from the mouth and walking awkwardly, emerged out of the blackness. She walked towards the brothers but did not seem to see them. 'She came walking strangely across Shoshone and came into Park Circle Drive and it seemed like she was a giant, and she came closer and closer, and my brother started to cry. Something was bad wrong with her.' As children, the boys could not make sense of what they were seeing in the way that an adult would – other than to intuit that something was very wrong. 'It was very mysterious, like we were seeing something otherworldly, and I wanted to do something for her, but I was little, I didn't know what to do.' David was mainly struck by the colour of the woman's skin which, as it emerged from the black void into the weak light, was the colour of milk. 'She sat down on the curb,' he recalled. 'I might have asked, "Are you okay? What's wrong?" But she didn't say anything. She was scared and beat up, but even though she was traumatized, she was beautiful.' He could not recall what happened after this, and the identity and fate of this woman is unknown – another incident of trauma lost in the void of unrecorded history.

This visitation echoes throughout Lynch's body of work, as if he was compelled to return to what this moment felt like and try to communicate it to others. A figure emerging out of darkness into the light appears in many of his films, most notably Laura Dern's character in *Blue Velvet* and Bill Pullman's character in *Lost Highway*. Lynch restaged the stilted walk of an abused girl returning to civilisation in the pilot episode of *Twin Peaks,* with the shot of Ronette Pulaski walking across the iron rail bridge. Isabella Rossellini re-enacts the moment almost exactly in *Blue Velvet*, when she appears naked and bruised on a nocturnal suburban street. In his work, evil repeatedly manifests in the form of sexual violence against women, but Lynch did not tell simple stories about a bad man who needs to be caught and punished. The abuse is typically presented as a symptom of larger and darker forces, outside of the light, which we struggle to comprehend.

David Lynch's *Charlie Brown*-style childhood in Boise was a golden time for white America. It coincided with a peacetime economic boom between the end of the Korean War and the start of the Vietnam War, and to experience this time of safety and freedom through the eyes of a child could be quite magical. Lynch portrays the white picket fences of small-town America at the start of *Blue Velvet* as a form of paradise bathed in the glow of goodness. But outside this light, he goes on to tell us, in the darkness beyond where the trees rot and die, there exists real evil. This is not the evil of bad choices or heartless decisions. It is an evil so incomprehensible to us that we can only experience it with the innocence and ignorance of a child. The feeling that David got when this woman walked into his protected world, a visitor from the dark realm outside, would haunt his work for the rest of his life.

The nameless naked woman with a bloodied mouth showed David that what was dark and secret could enter the light. And whenever this happened, it would be steeped in mystery.

3

One of the most striking aspects of Lynch's persona is his old-time mid-western charm and his purposeful, declarative style of speaking. This never felt like an affectation adopted to brand him as distinctive, but a genuine expression of his upbringing. It was the product of his happy childhood in a loving nuclear family who, along with their friends and neighbours, saw themselves as living the American Dream. He was hardly the only film director of his generation to have such an all-American upbringing, but while others came to see those attitudes as hokey or just not cool, Lynch never rejected them. It is hard to imagine the great and good of modern Hollywood using expressions like 'peachy-keen' or 'that was solid gold, buster!'

David Lynch's childhood was so wholesome and respectable that he attained the rank of Eagle Scout, and in that capacity he was selected to seat VIP guests at President Kennedy's inaugural parade. Each morning, his father set out to work wearing a grey-green, forest service ten-gallon hat, worn with a regular suit. As a child David was embarrassed by this but looking back as an adult, he saw his dad as 'totally cool'. The statue of a cowboy outside the Lucky 7 Insurance company offices in *Twin Peaks: The Return*, which so fascinates Dougie Jones, is based on a photograph of Lynch's dad.

The 1950s were such a pivotal moment in the evolution of American identity, as Lynch saw it, that they never really went away. His films and television series from the mid-1980s to the early '90s seemed to be set in a timeless era that was partly the present day but also somehow simultaneously the world he grew up in. 'There was something in the air that is not there anymore *at all*,' he said about the 1950s. 'It was such a great feeling, and not just because I was a kid. It was a really hopeful time, and things were going up instead of going down. You got the feeling you could do anything.' In time, Lynch would be seen as an oddity for his expressions of positive, folksy values and small-town sayings. By the 1970s and '80s, these were deeply unfashionable – to sophisticated city dwellers, at least. For Lynch, however, this was just who he was. He never attempted to portray himself as something that he was not.

Yet there was another side to Lynch, one at odds with this shining Americana. This is the aspect of Lynch adored by European cultural intellectuals. Here was a man totally dedicated to the fulfilment of his artistic vision, with seemingly little concern for success, accolades, audiences or getting rich – an attitude that appears quite mad to the mainstream American mind. This art-focused side of him is wonderfully apparent in a French television interview from 2002, in which the interviewer interrupts Lynch as he is working on a video for a music project. He appears topless, wearing only khaki pants, and is entirely unselfconscious as he emerges from a cave built in a wall of mud. He is covered in dirt and splattered with what could quite possibly be blood, but his hair, as always, is immaculate. Lynch is bathed in blue light and nearly drowned out by the clattering, ominous industrial music that plays throughout, yet he answers the interviewer's questions with positive, thoughtful answers, as if the situation was entirely normal. At one point in the background of the interview, a naked and seemingly slightly dazed woman with sharp black hair emerges from the cave. As a viewer, we can only wonder what is happening inside that cave but, in a typically Lynchian way, no answers are forthcoming. It is very hard to imagine any other American director giving such an interview, or indeed finding themselves in a similar situation. This aspect of David Lynch does not come from Boise.

The small-town culture that Lynch grew up in was conservative and hierarchical. It saw itself as rational, striving and practical and it celebrated sports, family and entrepreneurship. Many thought that it was a perfected society, ordained by God, and for a certain type of person with a certain type of mind, it could be Heaven. But there were many other types of people who found it frustrating and constricting. The limitations it placed on female agency, for example, led to Betty Friedan's 1963 book *The Feminine Mystique,* and the second wave of feminism that followed. The unquestioned assumption that white people were naturally at the top of the social hierarchy gave rise to civil rights movements, and the teenage desire to challenge the safe, boring status quo was evident in movies like James Dean's *Rebel Without a Cause* (1955).

It was not the case that young David fitted easily into the era that made him. He too was at odds with its stifling conformity. As his daughter Jennifer Lynch said, her father 'also despised all that goodness, the white picket fence and all that. He has a romantic idea of that stuff, but he also hated it because he wanted to smoke cigarettes and live the art life, and [his parents] went to church and everything was perfect and quiet and good. It made him a little nutty.'

Lynch's problem was not so much that this world held him down. He was, after all, a healthy white male from a financially comfortable family. It was more that this society favoured a no-nonsense approach to life, one that embraced rules, material acquisitions and normality. But Lynch did not have a rational or intellectual mind. He had a highly instinctive and intuitive one. How he felt in the moment had more power over him than reason. He loved atmosphere and texture. He would become absorbed in the present moment rather than think about the future.

This side of Lynch is evident in a strangely mesmerising 2007 short film he made called *David Lynch Cooks Quinoa*. It was a black and white recording of Lynch cooking quinoa and broccoli in a stark, minimalist kitchen while narrating what he was doing. In truth, Lynch did not cook often. As his assistant Michael Barile said, he structured his life so that he didn't think about where his next meal was coming from: 'lunch just appears'. Broccoli and quinoa is a healthy and perfectly acceptable meal, but it is not an exciting one, and few film directors would have considered making quinoa to be sufficiently interesting to film. Yet the appeal of *David Lynch Cooks Quinoa* rests in how absorbed he is in what he is doing. He remains entirely focused on the moment, regardless of whether he is admiring the quality of his pan or sealing the bag of quinoa to keep it fresh. There is no self-consciousness apparent in his actions, just as the characters in his films are never self-conscious. When he sits outside to smoke while the food cooks, he becomes so absorbed in telling a story about a trip to Europe in the 1960s that you feel like you were there with him. As his sound collaborator Dean Hurley recalled, Lynch 'would get so fired up about the smallest little things, just the simple act of life dancing before his eyes'.

There was no intellectual reason for acting like this. It

wasn't a rejection of any particular ideology or a desire to push back societal boundaries. It was simply how his mind worked. His attention poured onto the world around him with such force and persistence that the innate wonder of existence could no longer remain hidden. David Lynch had the type of mind, in other words, which made him destined to become an artist.

For most of his childhood Lynch had no idea that a career as an artist was an option, because he knew of no one around him who was an artist. When he discovered that Bushnell Keeler, the father of his school friend Toby, was a fine-art painter, everything changed. He immediately understood that becoming a painter offered him a way of life that suited his temperament in a way that more sensible careers didn't. That Keeler dedicated his life to painting 'thrilled my soul', Lynch later said.

Robert Henri's book *The Art Spirit* confirmed to him the rightness of this path and from that point on he only wanted to be a painter. Many people struggle continuously with the question of what they should be doing with their lives, but Lynch never doubted his path. '*The Art Spirit* became the Art Life, and I had this idea that you drink coffee, you smoke cigarettes and you paint, and that's it,' he said. 'Maybe girls come into it a little bit, but basically it's the incredible happiness of working and living that life.'

That his path in life was in opposition to the values of the culture around him did not bother him. Even before he left high school, he found himself a studio, declared that he was an artist, and started work.

4

Of all the ideas in *The Art Spirit* that affected Lynch, perhaps the most significant was the most controversial or radical – the idea that art was the most important thing in life. 'For me, living the art life meant a dedication to painting – a complete dedication to it, making everything else secondary,' Lynch wrote. Here 'everything else' includes other people. It also includes his own relationships and family.

Lynch went on to marry four times, having a child with each of his wives. His marriage to his first wife Peggy failed during the early stages of the making of his debut feature film *Eraserhead*. As Peggy described the situation, 'I had no doubt that he loved me, but he said, "the work has to come first." That's just the way it was.' Shortly afterwards he proposed to Mary Fisk, the sister of his lifelong friend Jack, who advised her not to marry him. As she recalled, her brother 'sat me down and said, "David is different, Mary, the marriage won't last," but I didn't care. David has this incredible love inside of him, and when you're with him you feel like the most important person in the world.' She would be devastated a few years later when he left her for Isabella Rossellini, just as Rossellini was devastated when he in turn left her a few years after that. 'David was the big love of my life', Rossellini said in an interview with *Die Zeit*. 'And I believed that he loved me the same way, but obviously I was mistaken. All my instincts told me we were a happy couple, but we weren't.'

According to his daughter Jennifer, 'There's no malice in Dad and he doesn't do these things out of selfishness – that's not it at all. It's just that he's always been in love with secrets and mischief and sexuality, and he's naughty and he genuinely loves love.' Lynch was always drawn to the thrill of a new romance, but he had less interest in the lengthy process of building a strong and stable relationship. The love of his life was Sparky, a terrier he owned in the 1980s. Sparky can be seen at the beginning of *Blue Velvet*, biting the water from a hose after a man collapses onto his lawn after a heart attack.

When the writer Chris Rodley asked Lynch in 2005 about being a husband and an artist, Lynch told him that 'I never was going to get married. I'd sort of perceived this kinda other life. I really wanted to live this thing called the "Art Life", where you're just in it all the time.' This commitment to the 'Art Life' was still evident thirteen years later, after the birth of his second daughter – with his fourth wife Emily Stofle. 'After I had Lula, he disappeared into his work, which is what he does,' Stofle said. This is something that he warned her would happen before they had the child. According to Stofle, Lynch told her that 'I need you to know that I have to do my work and I don't want to be made to feel guilty. Things change when a woman has a baby, and it becomes all about the baby, but I have to do my work.' As Lynch told the *Guardian* in 2018, 'You gotta be selfish. And it's a terrible thing. I never really wanted to get married, never really wanted to have children. One thing leads to another and there it is.' Stofle filed for divorce in 2023, fourteen years after they wed, although they were still married when he died in January 2025.

Lynch 'is not good at close relationships,' Stofle said, 'and it's not like he has a group of friends who he spends time with. He works and that's where he gets his joy.' This does not mean, however, that he has no time for people. When he is with someone, he is always intently focused on them. As Peggy Lipton, who played the diner owner Norma Jennings in *Twin Peaks*, said, 'When David looks at you, you're the only person in the world. He's never distracted, his eyes don't roam, everything is focused on you, and you get all of him.' This is why so many people fell in love with him. Lynch was always absorbed in the present moment, fascinated by what was happening and quite prepared to give all of himself to it. But relationships are more than the novelty of the present moment.

To selfishly dedicate yourself to art above all else is rarely the path to a happy, fulfilled life. More often, it leads to isolation, bitterness and anger. Those who withhold themselves from the world often find it a cold and lonely place – this is the risk faced by those who prioritise their work over the people around them. Their art is offered as their contribution to the world, but the world does not always see its worth. If an artist who neglects those around them wants to avoid an isolated, tragic life, they must be truly exceptional. As Lynch found his feet as a painter, he soon discovered that few others recognised as much value in his work as he did.

5

'All my paintings,' Lynch said, 'are organic, violent comedies.' They were dark, unsettling things, often mixing domestic or rural details with some implied threat or sense of dread. He used a lot of black paint. 'Black has depth,' he said. 'Because it continues to be dark, the mind kicks in [...] You start seeing what you are afraid of.' In other words, he was painting the world he grew up in. Or, more specifically, what the world he grew up in felt like.

Lynch had no interest in big themes or global concerns. 'A lot of my paintings come from memories of Boise, Idaho, and Spokane, Washington,' he has said. 'I like to think about a neighbourhood – like a fence, like a ditch, and somebody digging a hole, and then a girl in this house, and a tree, and what's happening in that tree – a little local place that I can get into.' He was dreaming up worlds on a very human scale, but this was not work that had obvious commercial appeal. As he said, 'You learn pretty quickly that a painting that's thrilling to you isn't necessarily so thrilling to others.'

For all that the five years Lynch spent in Boise were foundational, his family moved around a lot during his childhood. Born in Missoula, Montana, he also lived in Sandpoint, Idaho, and Spokane, Washington, along with a period out east at Durham, North Carolina. His understanding of small-town America is apparent in an early shot in *Blue Velvet* when, after showing romanticised images of the neighbourhood, he pans down through the grass of an immaculately kept lawn to show the writhing struggles of the insects beneath. As he has said, 'I learned that just beneath the surface there's another world, and still different worlds if you dig deeper. I knew it as a kid, but I couldn't find the proof. It was just a feeling. There is goodness in blue skies and flowers, but another force – a wild pain and decay – also accompanies everything.' This was something he was drawn to explore in his strange and disturbing paintings.

Boise provided the neighbourly bedrock in the Lynchian mythology, but it was balanced by the influence of a second place, in many ways its opposite, where Lynch lived in the late 1960s when he was attending art school. This was Philadelphia, a post-industrial city then undergoing a period of depression and decay. Here Lynch found none of the hopeful, optimistic neighbourliness he had grown up around. Instead, he was living among poverty, homelessness and anger. 'There was a thick, thick fear in the air,' he said. 'There was a feeling of sickness, corruption and racial hatred. But Philadelphia was perfect to spark things.' Lynch loved this dystopian landscape every bit as much as he loved his utopian suburban childhood, and he saw it as having an even greater impact on him artistically. As he said in 2019, 'Philadelphia is my greatest influence'. Although *Eraserhead* was shot in Los Angeles, it owed its distinctive visual aesthetic to Lynch's time living among urban decay. 'Philadelphia [...] was so good for me,' he said. 'Really, really good. Even though I lived in fear, it was thrilling.'

'What the average person sees as grotesque isn't to me,' Lynch said. He was obsessed with texture, something he found equally beautiful in organic and industrial decay. One piece of work, for example, was called *Fish Kit*. For this he dissected a fish and laid all the constituent parts out on a piece of paper, labelled as if ready for reconstruction. This was followed by a *Duck Kit* and a *Chicken Kit*, along with a simplified *Children's Fish Kit*. 'One time I used some hair remover to remove all the hair from a mouse to see what it looked like,' he has said, 'and it looked beautiful.'

'I don't necessarily love rotting bodies,' Lynch wrote in his book *Catching the Big Fish*, 'but there's a texture to a rotting body that is unbelievable. Have you ever seen a little rotted animal? I love looking at those things, just as much as I like to look at a close-up of some tree bark, or a small bug, or a cup of coffee, or a piece of pie.' Lynch's reactions to looking at textures sometimes suggest that they generate a physical response in him, not unlike that created by the internet phenomenon of ASMR videos. ASMR – autonomous sensory meridian response – refers to an experience somewhere between mindfulness, comfort and fetish. It is a desirable tingling sensation created, in those sensitive to it, by particular sensory triggers. Most commonly these are soft regular noises or whispering, but some people are equally sensitive to visual triggers.

In 1967, when Lynch was living in a run-down, semi-derelict house at 2429 Aspen Street, his father flew to Philadelphia to visit him. He was eager to check up on his son and see how he was getting on at art school, and Lynch recounted how this visit went in the documentary *The Art Life*. 'Near the end of the visit, I said, "Oh, I've got to show you some stuff," and I took him down to the basement which was earth and floor, really old, with cobwebs and stuff all around the ceiling level, and dirty basement windows,' he said. Down there, in the dim light, he had set up a number of little wooden tables, on which sat what he called 'his experiments'. These included several dead birds he had found and collected, a dead mouse wrapped in plastic and a variety of rotting fruit at different levels of decay. Lynch loved these 'experiments' in texture and organic decay and was eager to share them with his father. 'So then we went back up, and we were on the stairway, and I was ahead of him and I was smiling to myself,' Lynch recalled, happy that his father had seen the things that so fascinated him. 'I kind of turned with a smile as we were going up the stairs,' he recalled, 'and I see this pained expression on my father's face, which he was hiding from me.' Driving back to the airport, his father said, 'David, I don't think you should ever have children.' He did not believe that his son was sane or stable enough to be responsible for others. Neither David nor his father knew that, at that moment, Lynch's girlfriend Peggy was pregnant.

For Lynch, the point of this story was not that his father was worried about him, that objectively his lifestyle had become strange and disturbing, or that his family were concerned that he was drifting and failing to make a life for himself. It was more that he realised that his father couldn't see what he saw, and that disappointed him. Where others felt repulsion, Lynch saw a wondrous beauty. Why were most people blind to something that, for him, was overwhelmingly powerful and self-evident? He wanted to share what thrilled him with others, but how could he make other people see through his eyes?

6

The majority of Lynch's generation of American filmmakers were set on their path by a childhood love of cinema. The art form bewitched them when they were young, convincing them that making films would be the greatest thing they could do. This was not the case with David Lynch. 'Movies didn't mean anything to me when I was a teenager,' he said. That is not a statement you could imagine hearing from the post-war 'Movie Brat' generation of directors, such as Steven Spielberg, Francis Ford Coppola and Martin Scorsese, who spent their childhoods obsessed with film and filmmaking. It was not until Lynch was in his early twenties, when he was studying at the Pennsylvania Academy of the Fine Arts in Philadelphia, that the thought of filmmaking entered his mind.

Lynch was working one afternoon on a four-foot-square painting of a figure standing among dark green foliage in a garden at night. Suddenly he heard what he has called 'a little wind' and he thought he saw a flicker of movement across the foliage in the painting. It was as if the world he was creating wanted to move, and to live. 'I wasn't taking drugs!' he later clarified. 'I thought, "Oh, how fantastic this is!"' This fleeting vision was followed by the realisation that the medium of film could give his image the life that it craved. This was, in the words of his biographer Kristine McKenna, 'the core event of the David Lynch creation myth'.

For Lynch, wind was a byword for mystery. When he was directing Naomi Watts and he wanted her to act more mysteriously, he would tell her 'more wind' and she would understand intuitively what he wanted. Lynch's vision of a lost figure surrounded by trees swaying in the wind would, over two decades later, become the work which pushed him into the mainstream, in the form of his TV series *Twin Peaks*. When Lynch and his collaborator Mark Frost were asked to pitch a TV series to ABC, they went to a meeting with the network executives and talked about a murder in a small northwestern town. 'I remember David said something about, "And there's the wind in the trees." And he moved his hands in a certain way, and they all kind of leaned forward,' Frost recalled, and at that point, 'I kind of knew we had them.'

Lynch wasn't driven by a love of cinema. It is more that he loved ideas that required the medium of film in order to be fully realised. He found the process of working with celluloid to be useful and fascinating, and he was quite prepared to put in the effort needed to master it. But it was, ultimately, secondary – a means to an end. It was the idea, and how he felt about it, that mattered most. Film was a medium which would allow other people to enter into his world for extended periods of time and feel the sort of things that he felt. It was far more immersive than painting.

The American film industry is not designed for artists who are true to their creative impulses in quite this way. It is focused on working out what audiences want, and giving it to them. To do so successfully is a creative challenge, of course, but it is creativity harnessed into serving paying customers rather than honouring an artist's true self. This is why genuinely visionary film directors, like Terry Gilliam,

John Waters and Lynch himself, do not find the American film industry eager to finance their projects.

Film was a medium which allowed Lynch to marry sound and images and watch them play out over time. It was like manifesting a dream that could be shared. It was a place where he could set the atmosphere, direct the audience's gaze and make them feel as he felt. If he had hung a painting of the *Eraserhead* baby or the Elephant Man in a gallery, most visitors would have felt an immediate reaction of repulsion and quickly moved on. With film, we spend time with these figures, and in doing so we begin to empathise with them. By watching his films, we start to understand what Lynch sees in those characters. This is why it's hard to imagine any other filmmaker directing *The Elephant Man*, because the deformed character of Joseph Merrick initially strikes most people as monstrous. There are not many people who look at that face and genuinely find it beautiful – and very few of those are skilled enough filmmakers to make an audience see that character as they do.

Lynch's initial experiments with film were intended to be moving paintings, particularly his looped 1967 debut short, *Six Men Getting Sick (Six Times)*, which was projected onto a specially sculptured screen. Yet his short films expanded in ambition and led to him moving to Los Angeles to study at the American Film Institute. Here he spent four dedicated years working on his first feature-length film, so immersed in its world that he even slept in the set for a period when his first marriage ended. This film was quite unlike any other American movie before or since. He called it *Eraserhead*.

7

The East Sussex Psychedelic Film Club – or ESP-FC – is a monthly event I run with the electronic musician Richard Norris and the film producer Andy Starke. Films are shown in a seventeenth-century chapel in Lewes, Sussex, and we screened *Eraserhead*, Lynch's wildly experimental debut feature film, a couple of weeks before he died. Our *Eraserhead* night sold out in a matter of days to an audience that skewed younger than usual. I remember being struck by the faces of the audience members when they filed out to the bar after the film. *Eraserhead* is a dark, troubled black and white film about a man, Henry, failing to care for a strange, mutated baby. That it was made after Lynch became a father, to a baby daughter with a pronounced club foot, gives the film a disturbing autobiographical quality – especially when it builds to a scene where the exhausted Lynch-like father character cuts the baby open with a knife. By this point the film's dreamlike quality has tipped into nightmare, with the father seemingly disconnected from his actions, watching with horror what he is doing without being able to stop it.

Perhaps surprisingly, when the audience left the screening at the end, they appeared radiant, verging on the beatific. In theory this should have been a dark, traumatic experience, yet somehow Lynch's film had left people elevated.

Eraserhead demonstrates that Lynch was not an artist who struggled to find his voice. From the languid pacing, dreamlike silences and evocative soundscapes, he was distinctly Lynchian from the very beginning of his directorial career. Minor details of the film prefigure their more iconic use later in his work, from the distinctive zig-zag floor that would later define the *Twin Peaks* Red Room, to the photograph of a mushroom cloud on the wall and the use of lushly curtained theatre stages. His love of dirty industrial imagery, intense attention to detail and dream or fugue-like experiences were all present and correct. From the very beginning, David Lynch was fully formed.

This fact is helpful for assessing the extent to which transcendental meditation, a practice central to Lynch's life, helps to define his singular cinematic style. Lynch often talked about meditation and the positive effect it had on his creativity, which has led to a common assumption that the practice somehow explains the unusual nature of Lynch's work. His films are weird and transcendental meditation also sounds weird, the thinking goes, so it is easy to assume there is a link. But this idea does not hold up, not least because countless other filmmakers practise transcendental meditation and they do not make films like David Lynch. More importantly, Lynch only learnt the technique a year after he had started work on *Eraserhead*. Judging by the work he completed on that film, he was evidently cinematically Lynchian before he meditated.

Yet in a crucial way, meditation did change both *Eraserhead* and the films that Lynch would make afterwards. The film's minimal script was just twenty-one pages long. Its original ending was bleak and featured Henry being devoured by the monstrous baby. The first half of the finished film remains true to this script. After he began meditating, however, Lynch started to get more ideas for the film – the most significant being the character of the Lady in the Radiator. This is some form of positive spiritual entity with exaggerated, mashed-potato-like cheeks, who appears to Henry when he contemplates the warmth and security of his groaning, creaking radiator. She sings a simple, gentle song about how, in Heaven, everything is fine, and how everyone has their own good thing. In this hopeful, pure, innocent way she counterbalances another entity in the film, the Man in the Planet, who appears to be more of a representation of fear and control.

Once the Lady in the Radiator became part of *Eraserhead*, the theology of the film's world expanded to allow the possibility of positive emotion – something which had been sorely lacking before. When Lynch began meditating, he fell deep within himself and discovered something larger than he was, something good and hopeful. This led to a new ending for the film, one that can be read as an upsurge of love vanquishing the fear that had been controlling Henry from the start. The climax of the film was now Henry being embraced by the Lady in the Radiator in an annihilating white light – a moment of unexpected grace all the more overwhelming for occurring in a bleak, post-industrial landscape of hopelessness and indifference. It laid down a template for similar moments of spiritual redemption at the end of his films, from the angel who appears in *Twin Peaks: Fire Walk with Me* to the vision of the Good Witch in *Wild at Heart* or the return of the robins in *Blue Velvet*. Lynch had encountered a numinous aspect of the world. This was something that had previously seemed to him to be no more than an unlikely rumour, a tall tale as real as unicorns or fairies. He had started to tell a story of darkness, only to be blinded by the most unexpected light.

Had the film been as one-note bleak as originally intended, it seems unlikely that it would still be celebrated and screened nearly fifty years later. If Lynch's work had reflected the state of his soul back in 1972 before he started meditating, it is hard to imagine that people would have been sufficiently moved to construct an impromptu shrine at Bob's Big Boy restaurant after his death. Indeed, without that glimpse at the numinous, it is doubtful whether people would still be talking about Lynch at all. The notes of decency and goodness, so evident in his depiction of the townspeople of Twin Peaks, would not be such a prominent aspect of his work.

The sense of being surrounded by unknowable darkness would always be central to his films, but so too was the sudden, unexpected arrival of light.

8

Lynch was evangelical about meditation. His descriptions of its positive effects were not inaccurate, but it is helpful to think of them in the context of the intensity with which he felt things. Consider how he talks about coffee and donuts – most people would agree that these things are great, but even among the most committed admirers of donuts and coffee few people find them quite as mind-blowingly amazing as Lynch.

The same is true for transcendental meditation, or TM. Regular practise does offer the benefits that are claimed for it, but anyone expecting an earth-shattering explosion of cosmic bliss may feel disappointed. It can be thought of as the mental equivalent of brushing your teeth twice a day – it wipes away the build-up of stress just as tooth-brushing wipes away the build-up of plaque, preventing future problems escalating into something serious. Meditation is a regular daily event, and as such it soon becomes something familiar, commonplace and domestic – which is not quite the impression that Lynch's enthusiasm gave.

Like most meditation practices, the aim of TM is to quieten the mind and stop its incessant chatter – if only briefly. In other types of meditation this can be a challenging process, because the hyperactive surface froth of the mind does not want to be quiet. Transcendental meditation solves this problem by giving that yapping part of your mind a mantra to repeat. This keeps it busy, much like a harassed parent may give an iPad to a disruptive toddler in order to keep them quiet. The task of mentally repeating the mantra essentially hacks the endless mental chatter, allowing the meditator to sink down into a deeper, more peaceful state, relaxed both mentally and physically.

Normally, the mind is aware of all the endless thoughts that race around it. As those thoughts peter out, there are fewer and fewer of them to be aware of. At the point when all those thoughts come to a stop, the mind is no longer aware of anything. It is simply aware. The mind is not aware of any constraints or limitations, so it feels boundless and infinite. There is no awareness of time, so the experience feels eternal or beyond time. By this point there are no longer any worries or regrets, and there is no guilt or shame. In a deep enough state, the meditator is aware of a – typically very brief – moment of all-encompassing nothing, which is called transcending. This is a lovely thing to have in your day. It may also be why Lynch had very little interest in drugs, beyond a small amount of experimentation in his art school days. The stoned mind can seem foggy and limited to an experienced meditator familiar with a boundless state of mind.

The late Maharishi Mahesh Yogi, who popularised the practice of transcendental meditation, described this experience in Eastern and Vedic terms. He identified the experience of transcending with *Atma*, or the Self. Such terminology can seem off-putting in the modern West, now that the hippy movement has passed, so the modern TM movement prefers to utilise rational-sounding scientific terms. When Lynch explained what he experienced, he would often speak both in terms of Eastern spirituality and modern physics. As he wrote in his book *Catching the Big Fish*, 'The ocean of pure consciousness that Maharishi Mahesh Yogi talks about is also known by modern science as the Unified Field.'

Here Lynch is referencing the ideas of the physicist Dr John Hagelin, the leader of the transcendental meditation movement in America and also the president of the David Lynch Foundation. Physicists have been searching for a Unified Field Theory to describe all fundamental forces and particles for over a century, but they have yet to conclusively find one. Hagelin identified the unbounded state of consciousness experienced when transcending with one particular theoretical model of a unified field, based on superstring theory. He has, however, failed to convince many other scientists of this connection. Assuming such a field did actually exist, the great majority of physicists do not think that a human mind could become aware of it. The implication here is that the fundamental aspect of the universe is the same as human consciousness, which is the sort of claim that scientists feel needs a bit of proof to back it up.

That questionable claims about the unified field damaged the credibility of TM did not seem to trouble Lynch. He knew that this state of mind exists, because he experienced it most days. Hagelin's model for this level of consciousness would have seemed more plausible to him than the alternative – which is science not being able to explain something that he knew to exist and to be easily verifiable.

Lynch was, ultimately, an intuitive person rather than an intellectual one. He was not concerned about complaints that people could not rationally explain his films. He believed that anyone who paid sufficient attention to his work understood it on an intuitive level – much like how people understand music, and feel emotion through it, even though they cannot rationally explain what a piece of music communicates to them. 'It's absurd if a filmmaker needs to say what a film means in words,' Lynch once wrote. On a non-verbal level, the audience always got the film, even if they couldn't verbally explain it. As he said about his debut film, 'I felt *Eraserhead*, I didn't think it.' It was on this intuitive, sub-verbal level that Lynch's understanding of the world developed.

He was drawn to systems that science has rejected as irrational, including astrology and numerology. To Lynch, different numbers had different emotional resonances or associations. As he once attempted to describe his approach to visual composition, 'a bare room has a number of 2. And then when you put a person in there, that person is a *strong* 7.' The great many shots of numbers, in his later work in particular, were significant to him in ways that are sadly lost on the audience. He was also a deeply superstitious person. He believed that seeing his initials on a passing licence plate was a good omen. Travelling to the ABC office to pitch *Twin Peaks* with Mark Frost, he spotted a brand-new white Mercedes with his initials in the correct order, 'DKL', on its licence plate, alongside a number that had good associations for him. Based on this, Lynch told Frost that their pitch to the executives at ABC was going to go well.

After being interviewed by the BBC's Barry Norman at the Cannes Film Festival in 1990, Norman pointed out that Lynch's shoe was untied. 'This is for me a good-luck thing, Barry,' Lynch explained. 'About two months ago I noticed that my shoe was untied, and I'd had a particularly good day. Since then, at least until after the festival, I've decided to leave it untied.' Norman asked him how lucky he had been during those two months, and if he had fallen over.

'I've just fallen twice,' Lynch explained, 'but I was not hurt. I'd hate to think what would have happened if I'd tied that thing though.' Lynch then went on to win the Palme d'Or.

Lynch also believed in the existence of strange spiritual forces. He encountered one example of these when he was in London filming *The Elephant Man*. Wracked with insecurity, he did not know how he, a young, inexperienced American filmmaker, could capture the look and feel of Victorian England. He was exploring an old, abandoned hospital he intended to film in, when 'suddenly a little wind-like thing came and entered me'. That 'wind-like thing' gifted him the deep understanding of the period that he needed. After this experience, he said, 'I *knew* that time. It filled me with a knowing and therefore a confidence that couldn't be taken away from me.' A spirit like this, if we grant it the external reality that Lynch did, does not sound like a standard angel or demon. It is something else, something which doesn't really fit into many accepted theologies. Baffling inexplicable entities like this appear throughout his work, from the Mystery Man in *Lost Highway* to *Eraserhead*'s Lady in the Radiator or The Man from Another Place in *Twin Peaks*. The reason such entities are common in his films is because he believed such things existed in the world.

Lynch told another story about an encounter with the numinous. This occurred during a visit to the LA County Museum of Art. He turned into a long corridor, at the end of which a statue of the head of Buddha was placed on a pedestal. 'My eyes went up the pedestal and landed on the head of Buddha, and – BOOM! – white light shot out of the head of Buddha, and shot into me, and I was a balloon filled with bliss! I was filled with so much bliss, I had it for hours, this bliss in me.' After experiences such as this, it is hardly surprising that Lynch's films do not play out in a rational, limited material universe.

The importance of meditation to the work of Lynch, ultimately, is not found in his efforts to rationalise or explain the phenomenon. It is in the impact that it had on him, in terms of clarity, energy and enthusiasm. It is also important because the fundamental level of consciousness it reveals appears repeatedly in his work. In episode 3 of *Twin Peaks: The Return*, for example, Agent Cooper is cast down from a disintegrating Red Room into non-existence. At the end of his fall, he sees an endless, purple-tinged ocean that suggests this pure level of consciousness. Cooper's dialogue when he comforts the dying Leland Palmer in episode 16 of the original *Twin Peaks* was written by Mark Frost, but it fits well with Lynch's beliefs. 'Your soul has set you face to face with the clear light, and you are now about to experience it in its reality where all things are like the void and cloudless sky and the naked, spotless intellect is like a transparent vacuum without circumference or centre. Leland, in this moment, know yourself and abide in that state.'

When a filmmaker makes a movie, it cannot help but reveal their fundamental perspective on the world. Many current directors believe in nothing, and the extravagant spectacle they project on the screen serves only to distract, momentarily, from their nihilism. Others portray the world as a cruel place, a world of victims and predators with no possibility of redemption. Lynch hardly shied away from the darkness of the world, and he was prepared to take violence and cruelty to far greater extremes than his peers. Yet for Lynch, this dark parade was bearable because it is just the surface of the world. Underneath, existence is beautiful. At the fundamental level of existence deep within, all pain and guilt are annihilated and only a unifying love exists. The fog of toxic negativity and the noise and drama of life is just a filmlike illusion, a distraction from the immaculate unbounded mind below. This is the underlying belief that saturates the Lynchian cinematic universe.

9

Lynch never stopped creating. Even during the intense three years that he worked on the big-budget space opera *Dune*, he found time to start another project. This was a comic strip called *The Angriest Dog in the World*, and it ran weekly in the *Los Angeles Reader* for nine years.

Visually, each week's strip was the same. It began with an introductory text box that read, 'The dog who is so angry he cannot move. He cannot eat. He cannot sleep. He can just barely growl. Bound so tightly with tension and anger, he approaches the state of rigor mortis.' This is followed by a panel containing a drawing of the titular dog, who looked perhaps more like a black shark than a dog, snarling and straining at its chain in a suburban backyard. The second and third panels were identical, while the fourth and final panel was the same scene, but at night, with a corner of the yard lit by light from the house window. The only difference between individual strips came from the speech bubbles, which came from unseen people inside the house, containing unrelated snippets of conversations, strange aphorisms or terrible puns. Examples of these include, 'It doesn't get any better than this!' or 'I don't know why I like fishhooks, but there's something about them that catches my eye'. Lynch would phone through the text for the new speech bubbles every Monday. Regardless of what is said within the house, the dog is indifferent, trapped in a perpetual state of anger from which it can never escape.

The origins of the strip went back a decade, to the first year of the production of *Eraserhead*, when Lynch became aware that his constant state of anger was becoming a problem. He considered therapy, but worried that dealing with his demons would blunt his creativity. After being introduced to meditation by his sister in July 1973, however, he took up the practice and the constant anger left him – to the amazement of those around him. 'David was a lot darker before he started meditating,' his girlfriend at the time Doreen Small recalled. '[Meditation] made him calmer, less frustrated, and it lightened him. It was as if a burden had been lifted from him.' Lynch recalled Small reading a script he had written before he began meditating, and 'it made her cry because there was so much anger in it'.

'Before I started meditating I worried that doing it would make me lose my edge, and I didn't want to lose the fire to make stuff,' Lynch later said. As his body of work shows, the opposite happened. Constant, ever-present anger, he discovered, had been limiting. It froze him, trapped in endless futile mental circles, preventing him from losing himself in his work. Once the anger left him, he found space for playfulness and experimentation, and his enthusiasm for making things only increased. 'People think anger is an edge,' he said, 'but anger is a weakness that poisons you.'

This is not to say that after Lynch began meditating he no longer experienced anger. He could still be quick to anger and to raise his voice, as is evident in the behind-the-scenes documentaries on the *Twin Peaks: The Return* Blu-ray set. In a planning meeting, for example, he becomes angry at the news that he only has two days to shoot scenes in the Great

Northern Hotel. 'Someone arbitrarily says you got to do it in two days, that really pisses me off, it really does!' he shouts. 'We're always up against the fucking... I'm not working this way again! Ever! This is absolutely horrible!' Arriving at a set in the Nevada desert, his reaction is, 'This is a fucking mess. This is bullshit! You can't shoot a scene in that. That's a fucking mess!'

Examples like these can be found throughout his life. Lynch wrote about how, as a young, inexperienced director, he exploded with anger at Anthony Hopkins during the making of *The Elephant Man*, after Hopkins had reacted to his direction in a way he felt was dismissive. 'This anger comes up in me in a way that's happened just a couple of times in my life,' he recalled. 'It rose up like you can't fucking believe – I can't even imitate the way I was yelling, because I'd hurt my voice.' Lynch claimed that Hopkins tried to get him fired after he had screamed at him, but producer Mel Brooks talked him down. 'When it's inside you, it just comes out and you can't really help it,' Lynch said.

Lynch's 1997 movie *Lost Highway* includes a scene in which a gangster called Mr Eddy is driving along Mulholland Drive, near to Lynch's home, when he is tailgated by a driver. Mr Eddy allows the car to pass, but when the impatient driver flips him the bird, he loses control of himself. Mr Eddy rams the other car, forces it off the road, drags the driver out at gunpoint and beats him. As he does so, he shouts about the danger of tailgating and how the stopping distance of a vehicle travelling at thirty-five miles per hour is ten car lengths. That Mr Eddy's terrifying masculine violence manifests as obedience to the law is one of the reasons why Freudian interpretations can be a fruitful way to look at much of Lynch's work.

The scene in *Lost Highway* was inspired by the anger Lynch felt after being tailgated in a similar manner when he was driving along Laurel Canyon with Michael J. Anderson, the actor who played the backwards-talking Man from Another Place in *Twin Peaks*. After Lynch had let the abusive driver past, Anderson turned to him and said, 'David, you're a nicer guy than I am.' Lynch replies, 'No. No I'm not. I really want to destroy that fellow up there. But I just don't have time.' When Anderson saw that scene play out in *Lost Highway*, he had no doubt that it was Lynch's violent revenge fantasy.

Most first-hand descriptions of David Lynch focus on his striking positivity and innate kindness. When this is combined with the love people have for his work and his spiritual interest in meditation, there is a danger of viewing him in elevated terms, as if he was something akin to a saint. Lynch, however, was far too honest to make such claims for himself. As these fits of anger illustrate, he was just a normal guy who was as vulnerable to feelings of anger, rage, greed, depression and resentment as the rest of us. These feelings still arise in regular meditators, as vicious and as strong as ever. The difference is that by being recognised and acknowledged, rather than denied or repressed, they dissipate quickly. They do not build up to become a constant presence in your daily life, like the ever-present base layer of toxic emotion that defined *The Angriest Dog in the World*.

In a similar way, meditation did not cure Lynch of his mental health issues, although it did make them easier to live with. He suffered from suicidal thoughts during the making of *The Elephant Man*. He felt safer at home than when he went out and was always, to varying degrees, agoraphobic. The years he spent making a daily visit to Bob's Big Boy restaurant illustrate the extent to which a familiar environment made him feel secure. His sense of uncomfortableness in public was only increased by the level of fame he acquired in the 1990s. As his fourth wife Emily Stofle has said, 'David needs a lot of care when he travels. He doesn't like to call and order his own coffee, he doesn't want to be there when room service comes – that sort of thing. He's a happy person but he also has a lot of anxiety.' That he would spend months on set to direct a film illustrates the extent to which he would not let his anxiety stop him working. His insistence on always scheduling meditation time during his working day was part of his method of dealing with his anxiety.

Those who worked with Lynch would recognise those moments of anxiety and anger, but they would also recognise how quickly they would subside. Toxic sets and working conditions in the film industry have been much discussed over recent years, but there are no reports of any complaints from Lynch's cast or crew members. On the contrary, the accounts of how much people loved working with him, and how much they hoped to work with him again, sound entirely sincere. His faults were out in the open, unhidden. He made no attempt to bury them or pretend they didn't exist. He was, in other words, honest, and it is easy to like an honest man. As too many accounts of the entertainment world show, it is those who present as worthy, and who hide their demons, that are the ones to worry about.

10

David Lynch is frequently described as a visionary. The choice of word is certainly accurate, but this does not mean it is hugely helpful as a description. There are many different types of visionaries.

At some point in late 1980 or early 1981 Lynch flew from Los Angeles to Marin County in Northern California to meet with George Lucas, the creator of the Star Wars franchise. Lucas wanted Lynch to direct *Return of the Jedi*, the third Star Wars film. This idea seems, with the benefit of hindsight, to be entirely absurd. Lynch, surely, was too frightening a director, too strange and unsettling, to film this adventure romp with its enormous space battle, cuddly Ewoks and a speeder-bike chase on the forest moon of Endor. Lucas would later admit that Lynch might not have been a good match. 'I think I may have gone a bridge too far on that one,' he said.

Yet Lynch and Lucas had much in common. They were of a similar age and generation, having both been born around the middle of the 1940s. They both grew up in small-town America. They were both driven, practical and highly creative, and they loved machinery and building things. They found their path in life thanks to the newly emerging film schools, and they both made bleak, black and white art house films as their debut features – *Eraserhead* in Lynch's case, and *THX 1138* in Lucas's.

A few months after Lucas's *The Empire Strikes Back* was released in 1980, David Lynch's second film, *The Elephant Man*, was released. It could not compete with the financial success of *Empire*, of course, but it greatly surpassed Lucas's film in critical approval. The two men were considered hot and upcoming in the Hollywood pecking order, and it was easy to see them as peers. Irvin Kershner, the director of *The Empire Strikes Back*, had no interest in returning to the franchise, and as much as Lucas wanted his friend Steven Spielberg to take on the film, he was out of the running due to Lucas's complicated relationship with the Directors Guild. Lucas had to look elsewhere for someone with the rare skill set needed to make a movie like this. On the suggestion of Stanley Kubrick, he screened a print of *Eraserhead*, which he found 'bizarre ... but interesting'. *Eraserhead* might seem an unlikely audition for Star Wars, but *The Elephant Man*, for all its striking visual imagination, was not as self-consciously weird. It was a straightforward, easily followed and very human story told with great emotional power. The extraordinary make-up worn by John Hurt showed that Lynch had no problem working with prosthetics, and that he could treat monstrous characters with the sensitivity needed to make audiences care about them. From this perspective, the choice of David Lynch made a certain sort of sense.

When he visited Lucas at his Skywalker Ranch complex, Lynch had a headache. This built and built as Lucas showed him alien creature designs and drove him in his Ferrari to a salad restaurant for lunch, until it became something almost on the level of a migraine. Whenever Lynch told this story, he made it sound like a stress headache – a warning that the project was not for him. He described 'crawling into a phonebooth' to tell his agent that there was 'No way I can do this, no way!' His agent had told him that he would have made three million dollars from taking the job, but money was never the guiding principle of Lynch's art. Lynch just knew that this film was wrong for him. He called Lucas the next day and turned it down. He told George that he should direct it himself, because it was his film.

It's not that Lynch was against science fiction, or big-budget blockbuster filmmaking. It was early in his career, and he was still trying to find his place in the industry. For all the attention that his debut movie *Eraserhead* gave him, it also worried producers, who saw it as wilfully uncommercial. Since finishing that film, he had tried and failed to get his next passion project green-lit. This was called *Ronnie Rocket, or the Absurd Mystery of the Strange Forces of Existence*. His script combined the story of a Frankenstein-like young boy at the birth of rock 'n' roll with that of a villain who reverses electricity so that it produces darkness rather than light. When it became clear that no one would fund *Ronnie Rocket*, Lynch took jobs directing other people's stories – first *The Elephant Man*, and then an adaptation of Frank Herbert's epic science-fiction novel *Dune*.

In some ways, *Dune* seems an even worse fit for Lynch than Star Wars, given the size of the story and the complexity of Herbert's novel. Lynch's strengths as a filmmaker tend towards moments, feelings and mystery, rather than backstory, complex politics and plot. *Dune* was a rich, universe-spanning story that clearly needed longer than the 137-minutes runtime that producer Dino De Laurentiis insisted on.

When Lynch originally agreed to meet De Laurentiis, he assumed that it would go much like his meeting with

Lucas. 'I thought, Okay, I'll go meet Dino and I'll really get a headache,' he said. De Laurentiis loved *The Elephant Man* but hated *Eraserhead*, so it is easy to imagine the two men failing to connect. Yet when Lynch met De Laurentiis and his colleague, he 'got the warmest feeling from both of them and they fixed me a cappuccino that was out of this world'. For Lynch, the feeling he got from people and places was very important to him. When he looked at the story of *Dune*, he saw the hero's journey as partly a path towards enlightenment, and this appealed to him. Despite everything, it turned out that Lynch was prepared to enter the epic space opera game after all.

What is fascinating about the meeting of David Lynch and George Lucas was that they were both that rarest of things – genuine cinematic visionaries. It made sense that they would be drawn to each other and recognise the quality that they, but so few of their peers, possessed. Lynch had 'zero interest' in directing a Star Wars film when he was approached, but as he recalled, 'I always admired George. George is a guy who does what he loves, and I do what I love. The difference is what George loves makes hundreds of billions of dollars. So I thought I should go up and at least visit with him.'

Neither of them had a particularly romantic attachment to the world of film. While Lucas's friend and fellow University of Southern California film school student Martin Scorsese would work hard to preserve the history of celluloid, Lucas had no emotional attachment to it. He did more than anyone to develop and promote the digital filmmaking that replaced it, from pioneering digital editing to working with digital cameras, and advancing computer effects with his company Industrial Light & Magic. Lucas was focused on making things. He had no nostalgic attachment to the old ways of doing things if he could come up with something faster and cheaper. Lynch was the same, as his early adoption of the internet and his experiments with YouTube showed.

Yet despite their similarities, their work couldn't have been more different. Lucas had taken all his formative influences – the dream of escaping the boredom of small-town life, a love of Flash Gordon and early cinematic science fiction, the thrill of speed and working on vehicles, the films of Akira Kurosawa, and Joseph Campbell's theories about the structure of mythology – and transformed them into the first Star Wars film. This first film was an intensely personal reimagining of Lucas's own world in a way that later Star Wars stories, which were essentially reactions to that first film, were not. The power of Lucas's cinematic vision had such an unprecedented universal appeal that it changed the industry beyond recognition, ushering in an era of big-budget summer blockbusters and franchises. Lucas had absorbed his exterior world, transformed it through the strength of his imagination, and in doing so he changed the very nature of Hollywood itself.

Lynch, in contrast, went inwards. He looked deep inside himself and recreated what he found on celluloid. This had very little impact on film as an industry. It is true that the scale and possibilities of cinema as an art form were expanded by Lynch's work – film itself became bigger. Yet the cinema multiplexes that were built in great numbers during the 1980s did not become full of unsettling, dream-like surrealist films. There was no flood of new directors trying to build on Lynch's work, and Hollywood has failed to make a sequel to *Eraserhead*. After *The Elephant Man*, the industry essentially carried on as normal, its course unaltered, as if the movie had never happened. The film's impact extended to enlarging the interior life of individuals, and no further.

Lucas and Lynch may both have been visionaries, but their visions looked in opposite directions.

11

Of the two directing jobs Lynch took on after *Eraserhead*, *The Elephant Man* was a notable success while *Dune* was less so. Set respectively in Victorian London and on fictional planets, they were worlds away from the ideas that fuelled his paintings and his original film scripts. Both were complicated experiences for Lynch because, while he could fall in love with other people's stories, that did not mean that he fell out of love with his own.

For his next two projects, *Blue Velvet* and the TV series *Twin Peaks*, Lynch was able to return to small-town America where he was most comfortable. This personal grounding proved to be the missing ingredient that his work had been waiting for. In settings as deeply realised as these, he was able to balance his trademark terror and decay with a sense of decency and place – a combination that brought him a period of unexpected, extraordinary success.

Both *Blue Velvet* and *Twin Peaks* are set in small northwestern American towns surrounded by forests. Although they are set in the mid-eighties or early nineties, they look and sound more like products of the 1950s. The clothes, hair and the music tastes of the younger cast in particular are quite at odds with the contemporary world. Both establish their location with shots of lorries pulling huge tree trunks past diners. Both star Kyle MacLachlan, who played the lead in *Dune*, and who was also born and raised in the Pacific

Northwest. MacLachlan portrays a very Lynch-like figure – friendly, enthusiastic and respectable, but who is drawn towards mystery and investigating the hidden darkness of the world.

In *Blue Velvet*, MacLachlan plays a student named Jeffrey Beaumont who returns to his hometown after his father falls ill. In a scene deleted from the start of the film, Jeffrey is at a college party where he witnesses a sexual assault and voyeuristically watches from a distance for an uncomfortable period before he finally shouts out and intervenes. Jungian psychologists argue that it is important not to deny or hide from our dark sides, because to do so only gives them power. It is only by facing them that they can be understood, and overcome. This process is, in essence, the story of Jeffrey in *Blue Velvet*.

An opportunity for Jeffrey to explore his forbidden side occurs after he finds a severed ear in a field. Being a good, respectable kid, he takes it to the police, but he also begins investigating himself. This path draws him into a dangerous criminal underworld where he meets Frank Booth, a brutal psychopath played by Dennis Hopper. Frank is tormented by his love for the singer Dorothy Vallens, which he can only express through brutality and rape. Frank has kidnapped Dorothy's child, a situation he uses to control her and to also keep her alive, because she longs to die. Vallens also has a masochistic desire to be hit, because sudden pain is a release from the horror of her life. When the film was released, many critics were appalled by these aspects. They were unprepared for how far Lynch would go to depict real darkness underneath this idyllic town.

In one of the film's most memorable scenes, Dean Stockwell's character Ben lip-syncs to Roy Orbison's song

'In Dreams' using a work light that illuminates his face as a microphone. Like many of Lynch's best scenes, it evolved through his open working practices and a healthy dose of serendipity. Dennis Hopper's character Frank was originally scripted to sing the song, but it changed to Stockwell during a rehearsal. The work-light microphone was also unplanned. Stockwell simply found it on set and assumed it had been placed there for him to use, but this was not the case. No one on the crew knew how it got on set, or who put it there. Yet as Lynch intuitively recognised when Stockwell picked it up, it was the detail that made the scene immortal.

When Roy Orbison first saw the film, he was upset about how his song had been used. Although he recorded 'In Dreams' three years before the tragic death of his wife Claudette in a motorcycle accident, he had come to associate the song with her, because he could still see and talk with his late wife in his dreams. He would later come to admire the film, and even re-record the song with Lynch, but he was initially unhappy about the way *Blue Velvet* had taken his song from him and given it a radically different meaning. For Orbison, the Sandman was just a way into the heart of the song, which was the nocturnal vision of an absent love. Lynch's movie shifted the focus onto that candy-coloured clown. It made him a sinister figure who clambers into the sanctity of your bedroom at night in order to torment you with your desires.

In the film, Frank refers to the song not with its actual title of 'In Dreams', but by the name 'Candy Coloured Clown', a lyric from its first line. Years later, when Lynch was working in his studio with the composer and engineer Dean Hurley, he would reference songs like 'Mama, I Just Killed a Man' by Queen, or 'I Believe in Love' by John Lennon, much to

Hurley's confusion. 'I realized that the thing he remembers from a song – and considers its title – is the lyric that encapsulates the emotional pinnacle of the song,' Hurley told the biographer Kristine McKenna. 'That's kind of revealing in terms of how his brain works.'

In a later scene, Frank recites the lyrics to 'In Dreams' to Jeffrey before giving him a beating. Frank, his face smeared with lipstick not unlike the make-up of a clown, tells Jeffrey how he talks to him in dreams, the place where they are together all of the time. It is as if Frank has become the candy-coloured clown, the intruder that torments Jeffrey at night. Frank is Jeffrey's dark side, wild, unstoppable and released from his subconscious when he is alone in the dark. This is the side of Jeffrey's personality that causes him to creep into Dorothy Vallens's room at night.

Lynch confirmed that, to a certain extent, the character of Jeffrey is a self-portrait. 'I do see a lot of myself in Jeffrey,' he said, 'and I identified with Henry in *Eraserhead* too. Both of these characters are confused about the world. Many of the things I see in the world seem very beautiful, but it's still hard for me to figure out how things can be the way they are.' Lynch often wore a shirt with the top button done up, but no tie, and Kyle MacLachlan decided that Jeffrey should dress the same way, as an embodiment of Lynch. Yet there are aspects of Lynch in other characters as well, not just Jeffrey, and it is striking that the monstrous Frank Booth also wears his shirt buttoned in this same distinctive style. Indeed, one reading of *Blue Velvet* is that the confrontation between Frank and Jeffrey depicts the struggles taking place in David Lynch's soul.

Jeffrey is assisted in his investigations by a high-school girl named Sandy, played by Laura Dern. Sandy is represented as the blonde, innocent, good girl, in contrast to the troubled, dark, exotic, sexually available nightclub singer Dorothy Vallens. This being Lynch, however, Sandy is not quite as two-dimensional or blameless as that might sound. She cheats on her boyfriend, and it is her secret eavesdropping on her detective father that propels Jeffrey into the underworld.

Jeffrey confides to Sandy his struggle to understand why people as evil and unhinged as Frank exist in this world. In response, she tells him of a dream she had on the night that they met. 'In the dream the world was dark because there weren't any robins,' she says. 'Robins stood for love. All of a sudden thousands of robins flew down and brought this blinding light of love, and it felt like that love would be the only thing that would make any difference. I guess that until the robins come, there is trouble.'

The robins do indeed return at the end of the film, but it is only through Jeffrey confronting his own darkness that such a moment can arise. As Lynch said, 'The more darkness you can gather up, the more light you can see too.'

12

Lynch was constantly asked about his filmmaking process. Because his movies affect people in ways that other films do not, there is an obvious desire to know how he does it. Sometimes fans and interviewers felt frustrated by the simplicity of his answers. It was as if they wanted him to say something cleverer or more cunning, or to offer up a blinding revelation that granted them the secret of this great power. Lynch's answers were simple and honest. They were also highly revealing, giving us a deeper blueprint of how he worked than perhaps any other filmmaker.

For Lynch, the process started before the initial idea arrived. A film would begin, as he saw it, with the desire for an idea. That desire is like bait on a hook. You don't know when or what will bite, and you might need to have great patience, but eventually, some previously unimagined idea will be caught by it. Lynch uses a lot of fishing metaphors when he talks about creative ideas. He called his book on meditation and creativity *Catching the Big Fish*, because he equated ideas with fish swimming in an ocean of consciousness. Small, common ideas are easily caught near the surface, he claimed, but the bigger, stranger ideas that no one has seen before require you to fish at deeper and deeper levels. These ideas, it should be stressed, were not found during meditation. In a deep meditative state, the mind is aware of nothing – it is simply aware. Thinking of film ideas, by definition, was not meditating. But the familiarity with deeper levels of consciousness that the practice gave did help you cast your desire for an idea into the deeper parts of the mind, where rare creatures dwell.

How, though, did Lynch know when an original idea was a good one? There are many strange and unusual concepts in the depths of consciousness, but very few of them resonate on multiple levels or linger long in the mind in the way that Lynch's best scenes do. There are many surreal and puzzling ideas which, on paper, could be described as Lynchian, but which don't have the same impact and are quickly forgotten. It is here, I suspect, that many hoped he would provide a deeper insight. But for Lynch, this was not a question of critical evaluation or symbolic analysis. It was much simpler than that. He either loved the idea, or he didn't. All this was intuitive. If he loved it, then it was an idea he was going to run with.

An idea, once caught, might be for a painting, a piece of music, a photograph or even a piece of furniture. All these delighted Lynch equally. All would keep him busy manifesting that idea in a way that he could show to others. Film ideas were a rarer catch, especially in the later part of his life. Often these would take the form of images, soaked in feelings or mood, which suggested a larger story. To give an example, Lynch had been thinking about suburban lawns and Bobby Vinton's song 'Blue Velvet' when an idea arose in his mind, which he later described to the writer Chris Rodley. 'It's twilight – with maybe a streetlight on, let's say, so a lot of it is in shadow. And in the foreground is part of a car door, or just the suggestion of a car, because it's too dark to see clearly. But in the car is a girl with red lips. And it was these red lips, blue velvet and these black-green lawns of a neighbourhood that started it.'

An image like this is mysterious. It raises questions, such as who is the woman with the red lips and where is she going? Other ideas then follow, although it is not always apparent how they are connected. The next clear idea he had for this film was a severed ear in the grass crawling with ants. Often these ideas are connected more by mood than narrative. Sometimes these images may be unconsciously inspired by his deep interest in art history. With these first ideas for *Blue Velvet*, the ants on the ear are reminiscent of the ants in Luis Buñuel and Salvador Dalí's 1929 silent surrealist film *Un Chien Andalou*, while the visual image of the woman as little more than lips echoes a famous 1950 *Vogue* magazine cover by Erwin Blumenfeld.

'The idea is the whole thing,' Lynch wrote in *Catching the Big Fish*. 'If you stay true to the idea, it tells you everything you need to know.' His job, as he saw it, was to present that idea as accurately as possible to others. Ideas were things that came from outside of him, he thought, so he could not take credit for them. He compared himself to a chef – someone who did not create the fish, but who simply prepared it to the best of his skills before serving it to others.

Lynch's job was not just to accurately convey what the idea looked like but also, just as importantly, what it sounded like and what it felt like. All the thousands of questions, choices and possibilities inherent in filmmaking then boil down to whether something accurately reflects the original idea. This is the basis of Lynch's remarkable sense of certainty and vision during filming. 'It's weird,' he wrote, 'because when you veer off, you sort of *know* it. You know when you're doing something that is not correct because it *feels* incorrect.'

To make a feature film, Lynch believed, you needed about seventy such ideas. These ideas would typically be in dialogue with each other. Through this process, a narrative would naturally emerge once the ideas were arranged correctly. Sometimes an idea would only have a slight, tangential narrative connection to the rest of the film, but would still need to be included because it was integral to the atmosphere. The scene in Winkie's Diner in *Mulholland Drive*, in which a man talks of the fear he felt in a dream about the thing that lurks by the dumpster, is one such scene. Lynch started making his final film *Inland Empire* when he only had a handful of unrelated ideas. 'I didn't have a script,' he explained, 'I wrote the thing scene by scene, without much of a clue where it would end. It was a risk, but I had this feeling that because all things are unified, this idea over here would somehow relate to this idea over there.'

Crucially, what Lynch was not doing was reacting to a concept or a theme, into which a plot and characters could be inserted. That method is a top-down, big-picture approach to screenwriting, and its strength is that it can create focused, purposeful movies that are easily understood in marketing terms. Lynch did not have the usual fastidious focus on structure, 'inciting incidents' or 'character arcs', which screenwriting theory insists are vital. Given the extent to which an entire industry viewed Lynch's approach as technically wrong, his unwavering belief in it shows an admirable strength of character.

Lynch's process minimalised the role of the organising or rational parts of the brain. The result is a film in which events unfold in ways that make sense intuitively rather than rationally. Heavily structured films are restrictive – you can often predict from a very early point how the rest of the film will play out, which is not something you could ever accuse David Lynch's films of. His stories, where one idea suggests the next with no clear sense of where that path will lead, and where characters can become other people and the world can change without explanation, follow the logic of dreams more than they do the logic of narrative. They say more about the interior world of his characters than they do the exterior world. In the real world, a thing is just a thing and nothing more. In the immaterial world of the mind, a thing can have many different meanings at the same time, none of which is definitive and all of which are valid. As he said about *Mulholland Drive*, 'If you appreciate slipping into another world, like a dream, and if you can withhold many intellectual judgements and just float in the world and let it talk to you, you could have a very interesting experience.'

For all that Lynch's films have the feel and logic of dreams, he did not get his ideas while he slept. There is one notable exception to this rule, which is the ending to *Blue Velvet*. Here the climactic sequence of events – with the gun and the walkie-talkie in Dorothy Vallens's apartment – did come to Lynch in a dream. This, however, was unusual. As he said, 'Waking dreams are the ones that are important, the ones that come when I'm quietly sitting in a chair, gently letting my mind wander.' His ideas may have come when he was awake, but his stories are still the product of how our minds work when they are free and unconstrained by the immediate demands of the outside world. We may dismiss them as strange, but they offer a far more accurate portrait of what our minds are really like than normal films do.

13

For Lynch, ideas did not stop arriving when the script was finished. They had a habit of turning up during production, and even post-production, and he was always open to things that suggested themselves on set, in a manner that his actors found both unusual and liberating. For example, two of the most iconic elements of *Twin Peaks* – the demonic killer Bob and the otherworldly Red Room – were ideas that only arrived after filming had begun. Lynch felt an urge to film set dresser Frank Silva crouched down in Laura Palmer's bedroom, with no real sense of why he was doing it or how it might factor into the series, and in the resulting images, Bob was born. The Red Room arrived while Lynch was outside a post-production facility on a warm evening. 'We were out in the parking lot and [...] the front of me was leaning against a very warm car,' he said. 'My hands were on the roof and the metal was very hot. The Red Room scene leapt into my mind. Little Mike [the actor Michael J. Anderson] was there and he was speaking backwards.' Lynch did not know at this point that Anderson had taught himself to speak backwards as a child. Had he religiously filmed only what was in the script, *Twin Peaks* would not have been the programme we now remember.

Lynch had a unique approach to actors. When it came to casting, he did not ask actors to read for him, or audition in the regular sense. He trusted that, if his casting director

Johanna Ray had vouched for them, they would be able to act. Instead, he just talked to them and observed their innate qualities as a person. If they were right for the part, he would see it. Jobbing actors found this very unusual. 'I'd been auditioning for ten years and people could barely give you eye contact,' Naomi Watts said, 'but with David, he was just genuinely interested.'

After an actor worked with Lynch, they would usually emerge devoted to him and his way of working. Richard Farnsworth, who played Alvin Straight in *The Straight Story*, was speaking for many when he said that 'David Lynch is the most kind and generous director I've ever worked for. He's never got me upset and he's just wonderful.' His sets were typically happy affairs with a sense of playfulness and freedom. As Don S. Davis, who played Major Garland Briggs in *Twin Peaks*, said, 'I think any actor who's worked with that group of actors and with David Lynch as a director would walk over hot coals to work with them at any opportunity.' Lynch explained, 'If I ran my set with fear, I would get 1 percent, not 100 percent, of what I get. [...] In work and life, we're all supposed to get along. We're supposed to have so much fun, like puppy dogs with our tails wagging. It's supposed to be great living; it's supposed to be fantastic.'

Actors often comment on Lynch's unusual method of direction. They would rarely see a full script and often didn't know their character's backstory or the context for the scene they were filming. He would often guide their performance on subsequent takes with gnomic instructions such as asking for 'more wind', or 'more Elvis'. Russ Tamblyn, who played Dr Jacoby in *Twin Peaks*, recalled the direction Lynch gave him while filming a hospital scene with Agent Cooper and Sheriff Truman. 'David said, "Russ, let's do it again, and this time don't think about the words you're saying or what they mean. Just think about ghosts."' Lara Flynn Boyle, who played *Twin Peaks'* Donna Hayward, said, 'I remember, in the pilot, I did a very long scene that we had to shoot thirty or forty times. David came up to me and said quietly, in my ear, "Think of how gently a deer has to move in the snow..." It was strange direction but that's what I thought of, and it worked.' Balthazar Getty was struggling with a scene in *Lost Highway* until Lynch asked him to 'Imagine being a child and seeing a hummingbird buzzing around your father's head as he speaks to you.' Mädchen Amick, who played Shelly Johnson in *Twin Peaks*, has described Lynch coming up to her between takes, looking kindly into her eyes and touching her on the arm. Although not a word was exchanged between them, she then knew intuitively what he wanted from her and was able to give it to him perfectly on the next take.

When he was filming, Lynch liked to get as close to the action as possible, usually crouched down by the camera directing his actors through an unnecessary megaphone. When he was filming a scene with Bobby Briggs and Shelly driving in *Twin Peaks*, for example, Lynch was curled up by their feet on the floor of the car, telling them how to move. '*Wild at Heart* was such an intimate movie that he was usually sitting on the bed while we were doing our love scenes,' Laura Dern recalled. 'We'd have scenes where we'd get the giggles, and he'd have to pinch our feet to get us to stop laughing. He was always right there, always right next to the camera – very close.'

Lynch would often bestow nicknames on his favourite actors. He called Laura Dern 'Tidbit', Kyle MacLachlan 'Kale', Naomi Watts 'Buttercup', Mädchen Amick 'Madgekin', and Patricia Arquette 'Solid Gold'. A person in a position of power ignoring people's given names and referring to them by a name of their own choosing can often be a power play or a disturbing red flag, but Lynch's actors do not seem to have seen this in those terms. For them, it was a sign of intimacy and playfulness, based on a solid relationship of mutual admiration. Those who had nicknames from him seem very fond of them.

After David Lynch died, the tone and the depth of feeling in the tributes that followed from countless actors was striking. 'I love you & I miss you heart & soul', wrote Sherilyn Fenn. Michael Horse, who played Deputy Hawk in *Twin Peaks*, posted the tribute, 'I loved him and will miss him so much. He was my friend.' 'He was my north star,' wrote Mädchen Amick. Isabella Rossellini posted a very simple message on Instagram: 'I loved him so much.' Laura Dern wrote, 'I will love and miss you every day for the rest of my life.'

Lara Flynn Boyle spoke for many when she told *Deadline* that Lynch was 'the true Willy Wonka of filmmaking. I feel like I got the golden ticket getting a chance to work with him.'

14

While Lynch's films are typically expressions of his own singular artistic vision, his television series *Twin Peaks* is more of a group effort. As Lynch said, the series' co-creator Mark Frost 'is at least 50 per cent of it'. Frost had been a writer on *Hill Street Blues* with a great love of the investigations of Sherlock Holmes and the surreal, psychedelic British TV series *The Prisoner*, both of which became influences on the show. The music of Angelo Badalamenti is also integral to the success of the series, more so even than any of the films that Badalamenti and Lynch worked on together. Of the thirty episodes of the original run, Lynch only directed six and co-wrote just four. In terms of writing and directing *Twin Peaks*, the bulk of it was the work of people like Harley Peyton, Tim Hunter, Robert Engels, Duwayne Dunham and Barry Pullman. The cast all deserve credit for their role in the series' success, as do the rest of the hard-working crew. Yet despite all this, we still think of *Twin Peaks* as being the work of David Lynch. The world he created when he directed the pilot, with its own unique tone and atmosphere, is distinctly his.

Nowadays major film stars and award-winning directors regularly make prestige series for television streaming services, but back in 1990 film directors with Lynch's level of credibility simply did not make television. Most would have been embarrassed to do so. They feared it would be seen, in the status-fixated entertainment industry, as the desperate act of a career on the slide. This train of thinking, fortunately, was alien to David Lynch. Even after the success of *The Elephant Man* and *Blue Velvet*, he did not see himself as being an accepted insider in the world of cinema. He saw himself as an artist, as content to be painting, sculpting or playing with sound as he was directing for the big screen. From this perspective, television was just another medium ready to be explored. He loved working with Mark Frost, who was experienced enough in television production to guide him through the process. In terms of ratings, the network ABC were some distance behind their rivals, and they were prepared to take a wild swing and hope for the best. If a director as singular and credible as Lynch was prepared to work for them, then surely it was worth a try?

Even before a frame of film was shot, the fact that David Lynch was making a TV show defined *Twin Peaks* as something deeply unusual. As work commenced, it just got stranger. In the formulaic television culture of 1990, *Twin Peaks* presented itself as being as much an evening soap opera as it was a murder mystery. It was full of melodramatic emotion, a great deal of sobbing, and the complicated romantic lives of a cast full of young, very attractive people. Yet after opening with the discovery of a murdered girl wrapped in plastic, the murder mystery aspect of the show comes to the fore. The first sign that the show is not behaving as it should is the arrival of FBI Special Agent Dale Cooper who, in most shows, would be a more hard-boiled, world-beaten investigator who butts heads with the local law enforcement. Instead, Cooper arrives on our screens every bit as positive as Lynch himself – upbeat, enthused and impossible to dislike. Instead of battling the sheriff to establish status and power, the pair immediately become inseparable, with Cooper even playfully pinching his new friend on the nose. As the viewing audience encountered the town of Twin Peaks through Cooper's eyes, they too could not help but love it in the way that he did. It is Cooper's delight in small, simple pleasures like coffee, donuts and cherry pie that came to define *Twin Peaks* in the public imagination – the simple joyful moments of human life that the rest of television seemed entirely oblivious to.

Cooper differed from standard detective tropes in more fundamental ways. Ever since Frost's beloved Sherlock Holmes, detectives have been portrayed as fundamentally rational and often blessed with outstanding powers of reasoning, deduction and observation. Crimes may be committed in moments of passion and madness, but they took cold, meticulous analysis to solve. Cooper, in contrast, was like Lynch, an intuitive person, verging on being a mystic. The key to solving the murder was just as likely to be found in his dreams as it was in forensic evidence. Spiritual and esoteric concepts were sprinkled throughout the show, often divorced from their true origins. Deputy Hawk spoke of an entity called the Dweller on the Threshold as if it was part of Native American lore, although the idea is taken from the Western tradition of theosophy. The names of the 'Black Lodge' and 'White Lodge' sounded ancient and traditional, but they were taken from William S. Burroughs's novel *Cities of the Red Night*. Just before making the series Lynch met with the Dalai Lama, and this led to Cooper's monologue about the plight of the Tibetan people. As Cooper explained in *Twin Peaks* episode 16, 'As a member of the bureau I spend most of my time seeking simple answers to difficult questions. In the pursuit of Laura's killer, I have employed bureau guidelines, deductive technique, Tibetan method, instinct and luck. But now I find myself in need of something new ... which for lack of a better word we shall call ... magic.'

Mainstream television audiences in 1990 were not used to seeing expensive glossy programming that deviated from the average in this way. The way that it combined the simple joys of the everyday world with shamanic vision quests was unprecedented. The first series became – if only for a brief period – a mainstream cultural phenomenon. The second series, made when Lynch's focus was on directing *Wild at Heart*, stumbled and lost its audience. Yet while most television lived only in the period of its time slot, forgotten as soon as it was over, *Twin Peaks* was something that people talked about for decades afterwards. It lodged in people's memories, surrounded by a great wellspring of affection, an icon of a happier time. It changed the television landscape and laid down a path to the era of high-quality television drama that followed. *Twin Peaks* was so confident in its identity, so complete in itself and so perfectly realised, that it could march off into uncharted territory in a way that was otherwise unthinkable in the risk-averse corporate network world. The audacity of it was startling.

15

Criticism is rarely just a neutral assessment of the merits of a piece of work. It is typically part of a larger conversation about the contemporary creative landscape. It is concerned with the pace of cultural change and what particular artistic creations add to their medium. It is quite normal for works that later become seen as unquestioned cultural touchstones, such as *Abbey Road* by the Beatles or *Bleak House* by Charles Dickens, to be savaged by critics when they arrive. In a similar way, it is also common for work that is greeted with superlatives and awards when they appear to be forgotten very quickly. With time, the initial cultural assessments fall away. In due course, after their era has passed and their impact is evident, the true value of those works becomes recognised. The work itself remains unchanged by earlier attacks.

Lynch's work has typically only the vaguest connection to the contemporary zeitgeist. It was not made in competition with, or as a reaction to, any other filmmaker's work. It is subtly out of time in the way that it aesthetically mixes decades, which means it hardly ever dates. On the rare occasions where his films do feel like the products of a particular era, it is usually because Lynch was ahead of the curve. The central couple in *Wild at Heart*, for example, Lula and Sailor, now look like very 1990s creations. Presented like characters from pulp novels, they appear more like figures from a Tarantino movie than a Lynch film, and do not feel real in the way that Kyle MacLachlan's Jeffrey Beaumont or Naomi Watts's Betty Elms do. Thanks to the extent to which Tarantino went on to define nineties American cinema, pop culture-infused genre characters like these have come to seem dated. But *Wild at Heart* was not one of the countless Tarantino copies of that era. It was released in 1990, two years before Tarantino's first film.

In that year, after the launch of *Twin Peaks*, Lynch's fame and reputation were at their highest. He appeared on the cover of *Time* magazine, which called him the 'Czar of Bizarre'. He was in demand as a director of high-budget adverts for fragrances including Giorgio Armani, Yves St Laurent and Calvin Klein. He directed a teaser film for Michael Jackson's *Dangerous* video compilation, and he was awarded the Palme d'Or for *Wild at Heart* at Cannes. At this brief moment in time, everyone seemed to love David Lynch.

When he returned to Cannes two years later with the prequel film *Twin Peaks: Fire Walk with Me*, Lynch's moment in the spotlight was over. It is commonly reported that the film was booed after the screening, although its co-writer Robert Engels, who was at the screening, has insisted that this is not true. Lynch was no stranger to boos, indeed when it was announced that *Wild at Heart* had won the Palme d'Or two years earlier, at the height of his critical adulation, there had been a handful of boos among the cheers then – not everyone agreed that such a violent and wilfully strange film should be honoured that way. Yet even if *Fire Walk with Me* was not booed, it soon became apparent that neither the critics nor the paying audience approved of what Lynch had made.

The initial outpouring of love for the Lynch-directed pilot episode of *Twin Peaks* had gradually dissipated after the disappointing second series, the wrapping up of the mystery surrounding Laura Palmer's murder, and the programme's cancellation. Those who still thought fondly of the series remembered it for the good-natured warmth of Agent Cooper, cherry pie and damn good coffee. But at a time when the media was not prepared to face stories about sexual abuse, *Twin Peaks* had revealed itself to be about a father who rapes and murders his daughter, and this was the part of the story that Lynch's prequel film focused on.

Lynch's work is not for everyone. It is open to multiple interpretations, and it is prepared to leave questions unanswered. It deals with difficult subjects and does not flinch from depictions of absolute evil. In the early parts of his career, his work was something that only certain people were drawn to. It was something that you had to discover for yourself, and that made it feel precious. After *Twin Peaks* thrust him into the mainstream, he became someone that people felt they should know about, because everyone was talking about him. To encounter someone in these circumstances, after the mainstream cultural discourse has already decided they are special, is usually a recipe for disappointment.

After their brief period of mainstream adulation, neither Lynch nor *Twin Peaks* was in favour. 'Often there is something in the air that keeps people from seeing the work for what it is,' Lynch said. 'There's something else that's maybe not real that they're reacting to more than the work [...] I feel bad that *Fire Walk with Me* did no business and that a lot of people hate the film. I really like the film.' Over thirty years later, *Fire Walk with Me* is largely recognised as a masterpiece and Sheryl Lee's performance, in particular, should have earned her every award going. But the critical dialogue around cinema in the early nineties had fallen out of sync with what Lynch was doing. It was as if, in Lynch's words, 'I just had, you know, a bad smell. I couldn't get arrested in that year – '92 was *it*, man! Some stars were drifting! You just watch it happen, and you can feel it. It's the weirdest thing.'

Lynch, naturally, made no effort to change what he did as a reaction to negative reviews. He was not unbothered by critical appraisals, but he knew they were only very loosely related to the work itself – a poor tool for encapsulating something as rich, open and experiential as the films he made. A pattern developed after *Fire Walk with Me* in which every Lynch film would be released without fanfare, have little impact on cinema goers and ticket sales, then begin a decades-long process of accumulating viewers and building up its reputation. In Hollywood accounting terms, this makes them flops, but it would be perhaps more accurate to think of them as slow-motion hits.

In 2024, David Lynch appeared on the *Wild Card with Rachel Martin* podcast to promote the challenging album he made with Chrystabell, *Cellophane Memories*. He told Martin what he thought people's reaction to listening to the album would be. 'First hearing it – total bullshit. Second hearing – a little bit less. Third hearing, beauty. It just clicks, as being like a friend.' It is rare to hear such off-putting brutal honesty in a sales pitch, but it never seems to occur to Lynch that he could lie. Those with the patience to give *Cellophane Memories* multiple listens will, I suspect, find his description of it a fair one.

Here the album is not unlike his films, which can seem

difficult and wilfully alienating at first, but which become richer and clearer on subsequent rewatches. This type of filmmaking is something that Hollywood actively tries to avoid. It wants people to leave the cinema satisfied, entertained and feeling like they got their money's worth. Yet it is the case that every one of Lynch's films – with the possible exception of *Dune* – goes further up in your estimation every time you watch it. Each viewing reveals more layers and subtleties. Characters and situations that seemed baffling on first watch become familiar, comprehensible and pleasurable. Lynch's films are not closed, complete, linear narratives with one fixed meaning, but objects as complex, multilayered and endlessly fascinating as life itself. While many filmmakers keep things simple for fear of losing their audience, Lynch knew that people are capable of comprehending far more. That his films compliment the audience in this way is perhaps one of the reasons why they are so loved.

Lynch's brief period of mainstream fame may not have brought his films a lasting sizeable audience, but it did have a permanent impact on his own level of fame. An uncompromising, uncommercial artist like David Lynch was an unlikely candidate to find himself at the centre of a mainstream cultural moment like *Twin Peaks*, but being as singular as he was in manner and appearance, people remembered him, and found him fascinating. He quickly developed a public persona far beyond that of most working film directors.

It helped that Lynch was good on camera. His portrayal of FBI Deputy Director Gordon Cole is one of the most loved parts of *Twin Peaks*, and his cameos in cartoons such as *The Cleveland Show* and *Family Guy* were equally successful. It is hard to imagine his 2017 Netflix short film *What Did Jack Do?*, about a detective interviewing a monkey, without Lynch playing the detective. It is rare for audiences to accept directors casting themselves in their own projects like this. The cameos of directors like Alfred Hitchcock or Peter Jackson are accepted because they are brief, but longer appearances tend to take people out of the story. Few would agree that Quentin Tarantino's decision to cast himself in *Pulp Fiction*, for example, helped the film. Yet Lynch's appearances in his own films work, because they were so clearly set in his world that it makes sense you'd find him there.

The *Twin Peaks* audience may have dropped away, but Lynch's public persona remained fixed. He became a symbol of artistic integrity and life lived outside of commercial restrictions. David Lynch, unexpectedly, had become an icon, someone people bothered for autographs or just generally acted weird around. From the early 1990s, he had a level of star power that could eclipse his own actors. He became, in a sense, a way into his films – people would be attracted to his persona, and then go on to explore his work. As Kurt Vonnegut wrote, 'People capable of liking some paintings or prints or whatever can rarely do so without knowing something about the artist. Again, the situation is social rather than scientific. Any work of art is half of a conversation between two human beings, and it helps a lot to know who is talking to you.' The man and his work had become inseparable.

16

The all-American Eisenhower-era world view that Lynch absorbed as a child was not something that he questioned or challenged much in adulthood. This is something he has been criticised for. As David Foster Wallace wrote in a 1996 article for *Premiere* magazine, 'Except now for Richard Pryor, has there ever been even like *one* black person in a David Lynch movie?' Wallace was writing after Pryor had appeared briefly in *Lost Highway*. This criticism made no impact on Lynch, who continued to populate the great majority of his casts, particularly the leading roles, with white actors. Over two decades later, the almost entirely white cast of *Twin Peaks: The Return* stood out as deeply unusual for 21st-century big-budget streaming television. Of the more than two hundred speaking roles, only three minor characters were Black. That the most prominent of these was a naked prostitute did not help matters.

Gay men are also invisible in Lynch's world. The closest he came may have been Dean Stockwell's character Ben in *Blue Velvet*, who memorably croons Roy Orbison's song 'In Dreams'. There is no clear indication of Ben's sexuality, but his effeminacy is presented as deeply sinister. Dennis Hopper's Frank Booth can be interpreted as bisexual, not least because he smears lipstick on his face to kiss Kyle MacLachlan and threatens to 'fuck anything that moves'. Whatever Booth's sexuality is, it is violent and abusive rather than consensual and erotic. Lesbian and bisexual women do exist in Lynch's world, in contrast, most prominently in *Mulholland Drive*. They are typically extremely feminine, conventionally attractive and filmed naked or topless. Lynch was considerably more interested in female nudity than male.

There are also striking class issues in Lynch's work. These first became apparent in *The Elephant Man*, in which working-class Londoners are almost universally depicted as violent, cruel and threatening while wealthier and more gentle people are kindly and compassionate. In his American-set work, poor or homeless people are depicted as terrifying, especially when they interact with respectable middle-class people. Over the course of his career, they became increasingly dirty, almost to the point of blackface – such as the sinister 'Woodsmen' in *Twin Peaks: The Return*, who stop a couple in a 1950s car and ask, 'Gotta light?' The most extreme example of how terrifyingly Lynch can portray the American underclass is the memorable figure behind the dumpster next to Winkie's restaurant in *Mulholland Drive*. This homeless person, played by Bonnie Aarons and credited only as 'Bum behind Winkie's', is depicted as so frightening that they cause a character to seemingly have a heart attack at the sight of them. Some viewers have wondered if this figure should be interpreted as the Devil itself, such is the atmosphere of evil that surrounds them.

When *Blue Velvet* was released, Lynch was criticised for the voyeuristic way in which he depicted sexual violence and the rape of Isabella Rossellini's character Dorothy Vallens. The reaction was so strong that the film was picketed by protestors when it opened in London. Lynch responded by arguing that he was just being true to his characters. He did not agree with the assumption that Dorothy Vallens could be viewed as a representative of every woman. Thinking like this, in his view, prevented you from creating specific singular characters. 'Suddenly, if it's a Black man, he represents all Black men,' he complained. 'If it's a woman, she represents all women. If it's a kid, it's all kids. And they just go to town on you.' Speaking to the writer Chris Rodley in 1997, Lynch described 'political correctness' as 'almost an evil, satanic plot! It's a diabolical thing. It's this false way of not offending anyone.'

Lynch's way of working, as we've noted, was bottom-up. It started with an idea, and this generated characters that he strived to depict as faithfully as he could. Larger, top-down concerns, such as the overall depiction of women in American films in the 1980s, did not factor into this. He had very little interest in politics and, with the exception of *Dune*, his films did not concern themselves with the larger society outside of his characters' world. He showed little interest in interrogating the assumptions and prejudices that shaped him as a child, through which his ideas emerge. He believed that problems needed to be solved at the level of the individual, and he seemed lost or baffled by society-level issues that prevented this.

The question of why people do bad things runs through Lynch's work. As is often noted, sexual abuse and violence against women occurs constantly in his films. Typically, he struggles to condemn the abusers and instead is more interested in exploring what makes them behave as they do. Many of his killers and abusers – including Frank Booth from *Blue Velvet*, Fred Madison from *Lost Highway*, Diane Selwyn from *Mulholland Drive* and even the chicken-bothering monkey in a suit from the Netflix short film *What Did Jack Do?* – are motivated by love, albeit love that has soured into something toxic, jealous and controlling. After it was revealed that Laura Palmer was raped and murdered by her own father, *Twin Peaks* went on to redeem him. Leland Palmer was not responsible for his own actions, we were told, because he was possessed by an evil external entity called Bob. On paper this looks like it should be easy to condemn, but Lynch's refusal to fall into simplistic black and white thinking makes it more difficult in practice. After *Twin Peaks: Fire Walk with Me*, Lynch received many letters from young women who had been abused by their own fathers who were puzzled by how he could understand what this was like. As the writer Chris Rodley notes, 'Despite the fact that the perpetration of both incest and filicide was represented in the "abstract" form of Killer Bob, it was recognised as faithful to the subjective experience.' It is notable that Lynch-fandom usually skews female.

When Lynch thinks about society rather than the individual, he is noticeably less assured. 'It's nothing to do with right wing or left wing,' he said in the late 1990s, discussing the perennial belief that the world was going to pot. 'We've got to contain everything long enough to get a new plan, and that plan has got to recognize all voices. Maybe it means having the police in the streets everywhere for five years, just to prevent anything horrible happening while we get it together and make everything fair.' Arguing that five years of martial law is a reasonable solution is a style of thinking reminiscent of Donald Trump. Despite the two men having very different personalities, they are both people who are, ultimately, led by intuition rather than intellect.

Although he had previously voted for Bernie Sanders, Lynch told the *Guardian* journalist Rory Carroll that he was 'undecided' about President Trump. 'He could go down as one of the greatest presidents in history because he has disrupted the thing so much,' he said. 'No one is able to counter this guy in an intelligent way.' Trump then picked up on these comments, seeing them as proof that he was secretly loved by the Hollywood elite. He read them out at a rally in South Carolina in June 2018, telling his supporters that David Lynch, 'the great filmmaker' and 'a Hollywood guy', risked ending his career by making these comments. Trump, being Trump, mixed up Lynch's name with his own and mistakenly proclaimed to the crowd, 'David Lynch could go down as one of the greatest Presidents in history!' The crowd cheered regardless.

In 2009, Lynch signed a petition in support of the Polish and French film director Roman Polanski. In 1977, Polanski was arrested in California for drugging and raping a thirteen-year-old child before he broke his bail and fled to his native France to avoid trial. The petition was also signed by hundreds of actors and directors, including Harrison Ford, Wes Anderson, Sam Mendes, Tilda Swinton and Martin Scorsese. Emma Thompson and Natalie Portman both signed but later apologised and expressed regret for doing so. Lynch's signing of the petition led to a 'tough conversation' with his daughter Jennifer. 'I can tell you that after our conversation, he regretted signing it,' she later wrote on TikTok. 'He had done it for the wrong reasons and had ignored the horrible actions of an artist whose work he respected.' When he signed the petition, Lynch had only been thinking about the freedom and rehabilitation of an artist, which was in keeping with his individual-focused thinking. It took a conversation with his daughter to make him see beyond that and consider the victim. 'If you asked him today, he would not sign it,' Jennifer

Lynch wrote. 'I saw his remorse and found it to be genuine. Too late, but authentic.'

Despite all this, it is rare to hear Lynch's name in bitter culture-war debates. His individual-first intuitive thinking was softened by the striking kindness he displayed to others. His portrayal of the transgender FBI agent Denise Bryson, played by David Duchovny, in *Twin Peaks* is a good example of this. One line in particular has become beloved in trans circles, not least because it is delivered by Lynch himself in the role of FBI Deputy Director Gordon Cole, giving it a sense of strong authorial intent. Discussing how Bryson's transition had originally been mocked in the Bureau, Cole says that, 'I told them, those clown comics, to fix their hearts or die!' Lynch was not a person to deliver platitudes about the trans community in general, because that was not how his mind worked. His treatment of individuals, however, is the level on which he is usually judged.

17

When you watch Lynch's body of work you notice that there are certain images, motifs and tropes that he returns to constantly. Headlights illuminating an otherwise pitch-black country road is one example. Theatre stages are another, as are plush red curtains and mid-century furniture. Diners, coffee and cigarettes are all common, as are red lampshades, record players and room numbers. The black and white zig-zag floor pattern in the foyer of Henry's apartment building in *Eraserhead* reappears in the Red Room sequences of *Twin Peaks*, much like the framed photograph of an atomic bomb's mushroom cloud in Henry's room reappears in Gordon Cole's FBI office in *Twin Peaks: The Return*. That the start and end of his career both use these same images gives the impression that all his individual works are part of a larger Lynchian universe.

There are many other examples. Flickering lights are very common, particularly in moments when significant plot information is about to be revealed. Lynch's work, of course, always contains extremes of light and darkness. These are concepts that are defined by their opposites and, when Lynch turns on the strobe machine, he brings these extremes together, with the light and dark present almost simultaneously. The result is a level of intensity that is mesmerising and challenging at the same time. Along with his love of flickering lights, Lynch is also drawn to the crackle and danger of electricity – a powerful force that we live with but do not truly understand. In Lynch's eyes it is something otherworldly which enters our homes through mundane plug sockets.

While some of these Lynchian archetypes appeared in his work from the start and remained until the end, others gradually developed over his career and became more important as time went on. Doppelgangers are an example of this – characters who appear in multiple forms, often portrayed by the same actor. This trend began in the original series of *Twin Peaks*, after Lynch cast Sheryl Lee to play the dead character of Laura Palmer and regretted not being able to work with her more. His solution was to place the blonde Lee in a brunette wig, give her glasses and introduce her as Laura Palmer's cousin Maddie from out of town. As *Twin Peaks* had its origins in evening soap operas where evil twins or long-lost siblings played by the same actor were not uncommon, it was a slightly ridiculous move that still felt in keeping with the world of the show. Eventually, in the final episode of the third series, Lee would return again to play a seemingly unrelated character, Carrie Page, who looked exactly like an older Laura Palmer. While Laura Palmer was a victim of murder, this version of Sheryl Lee was seemingly a killer.

Lee would be the first of many Lynch actors who found that their role required them to suddenly change their hair colour to portray a second character who may – or may not – be in some way connected to the first. Patricia Arquette played both the dark-haired Renee Madison and the blonde Alice Wakefield in *Lost Highway*, just as Naomi Watts played both Betty Elms and Diane Selwyn in *Mulholland Drive*. Laura Harring also appeared both dark-haired and blonde in that film. She played the twin roles of amnesiac Rita and movie star Camilla Rhodes. The blonde-haired version of Laura Dern's Diane that we first meet in *Twin Peaks: The Return* turns out not to be real, but the true Diane appears at the end, with red hair.

Expanding this theme even further, *Twin Peaks: The Return* gives us not two but three versions of FBI agent Dale Cooper, including a fake persona called Dougie Jones created by the evil Cooper as a trap for the good one. Twisting the idea even further, Bill Pullman's character in *Lost Highway* suddenly transforms into an entirely different, younger man, played by Balthazar Getty. Here Lynch was inspired by dissociative fugues, a rare condition in which an individual finds their life so intolerable that their mind spontaneously creates a whole new identity. He was fascinated with the O.J. Simpson trial, and in particular the way that Simpson, who Lynch thought was clearly guilty, could continue with his day-to-day life knowing what he had done. All these dual roles, doppelgangers and identity changes feed into the dreamlike nature of Lynch's work. In dreams, a person can suddenly become someone else in a way that is entirely accepted by the logic of the dreamer, but which would never happen in the waking world.

Trees and forests are also key Lynchian imagery. Trees grow in the mystery of the wilderness, often to inhuman scales, but they also provide a primary material with which the light of civilisation is built. The swaying of trees and the feeling of mystery in the forest was one of Lynch's initial ideas that led to *Twin Peaks*. This town was home to everything from Margaret the Log Lady, who carried around a log like a baby, to conspiracies surrounding the Packard Sawmill. The image of a large lorry hauling a load of thick tree trunks driving past a diner is found in *Blue Velvet* as well as *Twin Peaks*. *Blue Velvet* is set in the fictional town of Lumberton, complete with timber-themed radio jingles ('Logs! Logs! Logs!'). For Lynch, trees are powerful symbols which can be strong or diseased, beautiful or frightening.

Trees hold within them the potential for another key Lynchian image, one possibly even more fundamental and mysterious – fire. Fire is traditionally used as a symbol of creative imagination, a transformative and cleansing force with the power to remake the human soul. *Wild at Heart* opens with a colossal wall of flame, the phrase 'Fire Walk with Me' became the title of the *Twin Peaks* prequel film, and the name or title of the mysterious giant in *Twin Peaks* was eventually revealed to be the Fireman. This inhuman giant was on the side of humanity, helping them in their struggles with supernatural evil. The actions of the Fireman suggests that there are spiritual entities who try to protect us from this great power, but fire is always dangerous. 'The devil took the form of fire. Fire is the devil hiding like a coward in the smoke,' explained the Log Lady, recalling how her late husband, 'a logging man', met the Devil. Where there is fire, there is always smoke.

It would be a combination of smoke and fire that ended Lynch's life in the end. His love of smoking was deeply held and unapologetic, but it naturally led to the emphysema that left him housebound and reliant on oxygen. In January 2025, an unprecedented series of wildfires burned across the Los Angeles metropolitan area, fuelled by climate change-induced drought conditions and hurricane-strength Santa Ana winds. They destroyed around 18,000 homes and caused 200,000 Angelenos to flee. Lynch was evacuated to safety, but the stress and the poor air quality were too much for him in his weakened state.

Many saw the Los Angeles fires as deeply symbolic, given the struggles of the local film industry in the face of home streaming, uninspired franchise offerings, empty movie theatres and film-friendly tax regimes elsewhere. The Los Angeles that Lynch loved, a place of light, potential and the romance of old Hollywood, was little more than kindling for this unstoppable inferno. Fire and smoke were transformative powers of nature that would ultimately escape our control – such were the symbols and images that Lynch was repeatedly drawn to.

18

The *Twin Peaks: The Entire Mystery* box set includes an extra feature called 'A Slice of Lynch'. The film features David Lynch sat at a bar, wearing a buttoned-up white shirt and black jacket with his hair as magnificently quiffed as ever. He is smoking, drinking coffee and talking about the one great regret in his life – how he bowed to pressure from studio bosses and solved the central mystery of *Twin Peaks*. 'The thing that kills me is that the murder of Laura Palmer was never supposed to be solved,' he said, placing his hand on his forehead. 'It's a huge sadness, a huge sadness, and an absurdity that that ever happened. There was room for so many other mysteries, but that mystery was sacred and it held the other ones. It was the tree and the other ones were the branches.' Lynch's voice goes quiet as he continues. 'It's just, like I said, a sadness,' and he trails off.

He spoke as if the wound was still fresh, despite the incident having occurred almost a quarter of a century earlier. He still believed that the mystery was the magic, and why anyone would ever want to solve it was beyond him. The sadness that he spoke of was evident in his voice, but there was anger there also. Whether that anger was directed at the studio, or at himself for obeying directions he didn't believe in, was not clear.

Lynch and Frost gave in to studio pressure and the killer of Laura Palmer was revealed midway through the second series. 'The pressure really, if you translate that pressure, was a need to know,' Lynch said. 'And that need to know is what draws you in.' Once that need to know was satiated, the audience dropped away and the series was cancelled. It is fitting that this footage appears on a Blu-ray box set titled *Twin Peaks: The Entire Mystery*. The marketing people who named it were promising that we would get everything, and that no part of the mystery would be held back. This seemed ironic in light of what Lynch had just been saying.

Mystery is a powerful tool for filmmakers and writers because of the extent to which our minds are drawn to it. When there is something that we are not being told, we want to find out what it is. Our desire to know what lies over the horizon, how things work, or what came before is inherently dangerous and frightening, yet it has fuelled human progress and taken us to the moon. It is the reason why the bestselling novelist in history is Agatha Christie. This fascination with mystery is a uniquely human trait which separates us from the rest of the animal kingdom. As a writer and director, Lynch knew how powerful mystery can be in capturing an audience's attention. But he is also as helplessly fascinated by mystery as the rest of us.

Part of what makes Lynch fall in love with certain ideas is that they are so mysterious. The ideas that he fishes for, and which he recreates so diligently on screen, often offer more in the way of questions than they do answers. Lynch wants to know those answers just as much as we do, and that spurs him on to get his film made. Sometimes those questions generate further ideas that provide answers, but equally those new ideas can create more mysteries of their own. His approach was to make sure that his finished films answered enough questions to hold together as a complete narrative, while still being comfortable with leaving many other mysteries unanswered. Sometimes Lynch doesn't want to explain specific parts of his films because he doesn't want to spoil them for the viewer. On other occasions, he would love to know the answers himself.

When *Mulholland Drive* was released, it had a reputation for being incomprehensible. 'I've seen the movie twenty-six times,' an American cinema usher said at the time. 'Every time I see it, I understand it a little bit less.' People enjoyed the acting and the atmosphere, but they did not think that the film, as a whole, made any sense. This reputation led to the highly unusual step of Lynch publicly providing a list of ten clues to help guide the curious, such as 'Notice appearances of the red lampshade' and 'Where is Aunt Ruth?' These clues came as a rebuff to those who claimed that his films were meaningless, and that he didn't have any answers to give. As he said, 'Mystery is good, confusion is bad, and there's a big difference between the two.'

Intriguingly, modern audiences do not seem to find the film quite that difficult anymore. While it can often take a second viewing for everything to fall into place, it is now generally accepted that the film does in fact tell a complete story, and an incredibly sad one at that. The film has not changed in the decades since its release, which suggests that audiences have become more media-literate. They have become used to stories that involve time loops or multiverses and typically have a better handle on non-linear narratives than they did at the turn of the century. Audiences, in other words, are catching up with how Lynch's mind worked. Certain mysteries are being solved. But this keeps revealing deeper questions and further mysteries buried within his films. As long as mysteries remain to draw us in, Lynch's films will keep being watched. As he said, 'Clues are beautiful things because I believe we are all detectives.'

19

When he was casting *Wild at Heart*, Lynch met with his chosen leads, Nicolas Cage and Laura Dern, to ensure they had sufficient personal chemistry to make the rock 'n' roll love story at the heart of his film convincing. On the night that they met, a beautiful 1930s art deco theatre down the road from where they were, the Pan Pacific Auditorium, was destroyed by a fire every bit as intense as the flames that open Lynch's film. As a symbol of their chemistry, this was hard to deny. It was also another example of the curious synchronicities that followed Lynch and his cast around.

In early 1999, for example, the actor Laura Harring received a call from the casting director Johanna Ray, telling her that David Lynch wished to meet her. Could she come and see him immediately? she was asked. In the panic of the moment, she had a minor car accident on the way over. Unharmed, she arrived at the meeting, where she learnt that the character Lynch was looking to cast would be involved in an LA car accident in her first scene. Harring got the part.

In 1979 Mark Frost, who was living in Minneapolis and working as a playwright, went to a midnight screening of *Eraserhead*. 'I walked out at 1:30 a.m. in the morning. I can't even say that I liked it, but it assaulted your sense of reality. I hadn't really seen anyone do that since Dalí or Buñuel. But I was left with a weird conviction that I was going to work with the person who made this. I even told people this. It's just a weird thing to pop into your head, and sure enough we were introduced six years later.'

Robert Blake, the former child actor who had appeared in films since 1939, was cast as the Devil-like Mystery Man in *Lost Highway*. The arrival of this disturbing figure causes Bill Pullman's character to seemingly kill his wife, before entering into a psychogenic fugue in order to protect himself from the memory of his actions. Four years later, Blake was arrested after his second wife was murdered and, like Pullman's character, he insisted he was innocent. He was acquitted in court but found liable for her wrongful death in a civil case eight months later, brought by the murdered woman's children. Quentin Tarantino's novelisation of his film *Once Upon a Time in Hollywood* was dedicated to Blake, as well as other Hollywood 'old timers'. The story is about a stuntman, Cliff Booth, who may or may not have murdered his wife.

There was a great deal of tragedy around the deaths of many of Lynch's collaborators. The contributions of the singer Julee Cruise to the *Twin Peaks* soundtrack were an integral part of the programme's atmosphere but, struggling with unbearable pain caused by an autoimmune disease, she took her own life in 2022. Frank Silva, the actor and set dresser best known for playing the evil entity Bob in *Twin Peaks*, died from AIDS-related complications in 1995 after a period of homelessness and depression. Peter Ivers, the musician who worked on *Eraserhead* and wrote the lyrics for the Lady in the Radiator song 'In Heaven', was beaten to death with a hammer in a Los Angeles apartment. The identity of his murderer was never proven, but the murder has generated countless theories over the years.

Equally tragic were the later years of Jack Nance, the actor most closely associated with Lynch, having appeared in most of his major work from *Eraserhead* to *Lost Highway*. Nance called his troubled wife Kelly Jean Van Dyke from a movie set in 1991, and she threatened to kill herself if Nance hung up on her. At that moment, a lightning storm knocked out the telephone wires. In response, his wife hanged herself. Nance had always struggled with alcohol use and, following her death, he began drinking again. This led to two strokes and a period of deep depression. He died in 1996 following a blow to the head received in a fight in the street. In a perfectly Lynchian detail, the brawl took place outside a donut shop.

There are some exceptions, but most of the actors that Lynch worked with are now primarily remembered for their appearances in his films. It is as if when you fall into that world, you can never leave it, even if you want to. The Lynchian world can be a disturbing one to get lost in.

20

In 2005, Lynch established the David Lynch Foundation – or, to give it its full name, The David Lynch Foundation for Consciousness-Based Education and World Peace. Its goal is to make transcendental meditation freely available to the traumatised or disadvantaged members of society who are most in need of it. These include veterans struggling with PTSD, refugees and asylum seekers, overstressed healthcare workers, prisoners, children in inner-city schools, and women and girls who are victims of abuse. Knowing how powerful the impact of this practice was on his own life, Lynch viewed it as a proven method to reduce the amount of suffering in the world, albeit at the rate of one mind at a time. This was in keeping with his understanding of problems as being something that arose on the level of individuals, not on the level of society.

Lynch also had several other beliefs and practices that he did not promote in such a public way. He believed in astrology and numerology, for example, but he never tried to publicly promote these systems of thought to others. He became a vegetarian in the early 1970s, but he did not speak about his reasons or the benefits of the diet in interviews. Here he differs from the surviving Beatles Paul McCartney and Ringo Starr, who have helped him promote the David Lynch Foundation. The surviving Beatles support vegetarianism very publicly – most notably with the establishment of McCartney's 'Meat Free Monday' campaign in 2009. Admittedly, how seriously Lynch took vegetarianism is not entirely clear, given his fondness for tuna melts. As Raffaella De Laurentiis, the producer of *Dune*, recalled, 'David was a vegetarian then, but he loved pâté, and I remember he was always having foie gras.'

If Lynch could be said to have promoted any particular diet, it was an unhealthy one. The things he chose to celebrate publicly were nicotine, sugar and caffeine. *Twin Peaks* could sometimes seem like an extended advert for the joys of coffee, and its donut budget must have been considerable. 'I'm heavily into sugar,' he once said. 'I call it "granulated happiness." It's just a great help. You know, a friend.'

It was Lynch's love of coffee and sugar that led to him visiting the same branch of Bob's Big Boy restaurant every day at around 2.30 p.m. for about seven years. Here he would always order a silver goblet chocolate milkshake and a cup of coffee. The sugar from the milkshake would inspire him, and he'd write down the ideas that followed on the napkins provided. This routine became so central to Lynch-lore that, after he died, the mascot outside the Bob's Big Boy in Burbank became the site of the spontaneous public shrine mentioned earlier.

Cigarettes were also integral to his life. He started when he was eight and smoked heavily for the next sixty-seven years. Smoking was unusual in Hollywood and the actor Michael Cera, when he first met Lynch, recalled being startled by his yellowing teeth. When Lynch was diagnosed with emphysema, a disease that would ultimately leave him housebound and in need of supplementary oxygen, he did not immediately quit smoking. Here was an echo of a scene in *The Straight Story*, a film he made two decades earlier. After the main character is diagnosed with emphysema, Lynch cut to him lighting a cigar. Yet the progression of the disease and the state of his lungs meant that, two years later, Lynch had no choice but to quit. As he told *People* magazine in November 2024, two months before he died, 'I can hardly walk across a room. It's like you're walking around with a plastic bag around your head.'

Yet even when he publicly announced his condition in August 2024, his love of smoking was still evident. As he wrote on social media, 'Yes, I have emphysema from my many years of smoking. I have to say that I enjoyed smoking very much, and I do love tobacco – the smell of it, lighting cigarettes on fire, smoking them – but there is a price to pay for this enjoyment, and the price for me is emphysema [...] I am filled with happiness, and I will never retire.'

Just as sugar and caffeine helped his creative processes, so too was smoking a key part of his practice as an artist. 'I loved the smell of tobacco, the taste of tobacco,' he said after he quit, 'I loved lighting cigarettes. It was part of being a painter and a filmmaker for me.'

There was a pattern, then, to the aspects of his life that he actively promoted. Sugar, nicotine and caffeine may seem very different to meditation but they were all, in Lynch's mind, sources of energy. They powered his imagination and kept him creative. Lynch's enthusiasm for 'damn good coffee', a sugar rush or transcendental meditation-induced clarity may appear like a strange collection of unrelated quirks, but they all point to his desire to share the best part of his life. They were the fuel that allowed him to capture the ideas that he found so beautiful. The act of exercising his creative imagination was always David Lynch's greatest pleasure.

21

The existence of *Twin Peaks: The Return* is something of a miracle. Nothing remotely like it had been made before, and it seems unlikely that anything like it will ever be made again. It blossomed in a brief moment when television networks, in competition with newly formed streaming companies, were prepared to spend unsustainably vast sums to attract market share. That the network Showtime would take such a financial risk on David Lynch, giving him final cut and trusting him to deliver a quality series without any creative control on their part, was a remarkable act of faith and not something that happened often in his life. While the final budget is unknown, we can be sure it was greater than $41 million, and some estimates suggest that $80 million seems possible. Adjusting for inflation, this was the largest budget Lynch had worked with since *Dune*.

When filming began in 2015, it had been fourteen years since the release of *Mulholland Drive* – an enigmatic film that delivered its mysteries through beautiful romantic cinematography that recalled Hollywood's Golden Age. After *Mulholland Drive*, however, curiosity and necessity had pushed Lynch to reject that style of polished, professional filmmaking. He turned, instead, to cheap, amateur-looking digital video cameras, which produced an aesthetic every bit as disjointed and disturbing as his narratives. The low-budget experimental short films that he made for his pioneering website, such as *DumbLand, Rabbits* and *Out Yonder*, were a tough watch even for the most dedicated Lynchian.

Lynch's final feature film, *Inland Empire*, was shot with a low-resolution early digital camera using an auto-focus feature that struggled in Lynch's low lighting. He was not unaware that it looked like shit, it's just that he, perhaps alone, found the aesthetic interesting. When he premiered *Inland Empire*, the result was not unlike the time he showed his father his collection of rotting birds in his Philadelphia basement, in the hope that he would like them. Lynch was, once again, insisting that something incredibly ugly was visually fascinating.

Lynch's best work had always been meticulous. In his twentieth-century work, each shot was a product of devotion, time and a sufficient amount of money required to realise it properly. The Lynch that Showtime took a chance on was, in contrast, someone who, for over a decade, had produced work that looked amateurish and self-indulgent, at first glance at least. If he had delivered a *Twin Peaks* series in the style of *Inland Empire*, it would not have gone down well. Yet such was the love and affection that people still felt for the original series, and the credibility that Lynch had maintained over the years, that Showtime took a chance on him.

The announcement that *Twin Peaks* was returning was typically enigmatic. At exactly the same time – 11.30 a.m. on 3 October 2014 – Mark Frost and David Lynch both tweeted the phrase 'Dear Twitter Friends: That gum you like is going to come back in style #damngoodcoffee'. This was enough for the news to go viral. As a story, *Twin Peaks: The Return* was justified narratively by a strange statement that Agent Cooper was told when he first encountered the

Red Room, back in the third episode of the first series. 'I'll see you again in twenty-five years,' Laura Palmer told him, speaking backwards. Few people realised then that she was also speaking prophecy.

At that point, it wasn't clear how long the series would be. Showtime's initial announcement claimed it would run for nine episodes, but this was news to Lynch. For a number of years Lynch and Frost had secretly been working on what turned out to be a 334-page script. They delivered their script to Showtime on a Friday and told them, in a fit of showmanship, that if they wanted the show they had to let them know by Monday. When the response came back 'yes', Frost moved off the project to write a pair of lore-heavy books that bookend the series, *The Secret History of Twin Peaks* and *Twin Peaks: The Final Dossier*. These books tie the *Twin Peaks* mythos into centuries of American folklore and conspiracy theory, from the Lewis and Clark Expedition to the Roswell UFO incident, creating a grand synthesis of American Mystery. Lynch, meanwhile, continued to work on the script by himself, adding new ideas as they came to him.

Lynch was not concerned about how many episodes the series would run to. This was not something he was expecting to find out until he got to the edit room. However, his approach was problematic for Showtime, whose entire budgeting system was structured around the cost per episode. It led to a public standoff in which Lynch threatened to walk away from the project before the two sides thankfully came to an agreement. Lynch eventually delivered eighteen hour-long episodes, the equivalent of seven or eight feature films, far more than anyone had been expecting. This made the series great value for money, from the perspective of Showtime's spreadsheets.

The shoot ran for one hundred and forty long days and required the seventy-year-old Lynch to work between twelve and seventeen hours a day. As his assistant Michael Barile told Kristine McKenna, 'He got sick several times, and there were a few days when he had crap in his lungs and a fever and could barely get upstairs when we dropped him off. But there he'd be six hours later, up and back for work.' As Lynch's wife Emily Stofle recalled, 'At one point he said to me, "Puff, I was in my trailer meditating and I fell asleep and when I woke up I didn't know where I was. Everyone on the set is younger than me and I'm so tired." He got really sick but he never stopped working.' Yet despite all this, the behind-the-scenes footage of *Twin Peaks: The Return* shows Lynch completely focused on what he is doing and who he is talking to. He had a diamond-clear understanding of each scene and what he required of his actors, and displayed his usual dedication to creating a happy, playful, creative atmosphere. For the huge, two hundred-plus cast, and especially the twenty-seven actors who returned from the original series, working with Lynch again in this atmosphere was what acting was all about.

Although the finished work was undoubtedly an eighteen-part television series, it did not feel like any television series before or since. For some people, it had transcended the small screen to such an extent that it made more sense to think of it as a very, very long film. *Sight and Sound* and the French magazine *Cahiers du Cinéma* both classed it as a film, perhaps out of a desire to include it in their end of year 'Best Film' lists. Lynch screened the first two episodes at Cannes, where it received a lengthy standing ovation.

Twin Peaks: The Return was an exercise in deliberately not giving the audience what they wanted or expected.

The power of nostalgia wanted to see peppy Special Agent Dale Cooper return to the troubled but essentially decent town of Twin Peaks and punish wrongdoers. Lynch avoided doing this throughout the first sixteen episodes, taking the viewers on a completely different journey that they were in no way prepared for. He also avoided recreating the 1950s-style romanticised atmosphere of the original series, offering a vision of *Twin Peaks* that was firmly planted in the twenty-first century. The viewer had no choice but to forget their preconceived notions of what they wanted, and surrender to the confidence of Frost and Lynch's new story. They had to allow themselves to be swept along into previously unimagined territory, and few were prepared for the places that the series took them. The title of the positive review on *Deadline* was simply, 'Twin Peaks Review: WTF Was That?'

What it was, was essentially a summation of Lynch's entire career. It incorporated all the tropes he had developed over the years, from doppelgangers to flickering lights and the atmosphere of the woods at night. It included all his favourite actors and collaborators, including Kyle MacLachlan, Laura Dern, Harry Dean Stanton and Naomi Watts. It was, in places, more of an experimental art house film than even *Eraserhead*, not least in the lengthy dialogue-free sections of episode 8 which linked the otherworldly evil that haunted Twin Peaks with the creation of the atom bomb and the birth of rock 'n' roll. As baffling as parts of it might have appeared initially, it was far from incomprehensible, as a second or perhaps third watch made clear. Mesmerising, unequalled and extraordinarily ambitious, it was Lynch taking advantage of a brief window in the entertainment ecosystem to express the ideas that he caught and fell in love with more fully than he had ever done before. It stands as the capstone to his career, proof that he lived up to the potential inherent in his dedication to the Art Life. It is one of the most remarkable creative achievements of the twenty-first century.

22

When most filmmakers want their audience to feel an emotion, their usual method of achieving this is to display a performance of that emotion on screen. Here they are taking advantage of what are called 'mirror neurons' in the brain – neurons that fire in sympathy with someone being observed in a way that mimics, in the mind of the observer, what that other person is going through. Mirror neurons play an important role in feeling empathy, learning skills and understanding the intent of others. That filmmakers can use them to generate a desired emotion in an audience is just a happy by-product of many thousands of years of evolution.

For example, if a filmmaker wants their audience to feel triumphant, they could show us a likeable character with frustrated ambitions and then show us their delight when their dreams come true. This would cause the mirror neurons of the audience watching to fire in sympathy, generating an echo of the emotion depicted on screen in the minds of the audience. This approach is similar to techniques employed by the advertising industry, where the viewer's brain chemistry can be used to manipulate them into buying a product they might otherwise have had no interest in.

Mirror neurons are an integral part of all storytelling, but Lynch's work is less reliant on them than other filmmakers. Instead, his approach was more focused on putting the audience into a state more akin to mindfulness than exhilaration.

He wanted those watching to experience the present moment as profoundly as he did. To do this he was always trying to slow things down on screen. He left long pauses in conversations, and he basically jammed a spanner into the headlong rush into the future that is the default pacing of Hollywood filmmaking. It's impossible to imagine any other director giving us the scene in *Twin Peaks: The Return*, episode 7, in which a character is filmed in a single locked-off shot sweeping the floor for two and a half minutes. Most filmmakers would fear that such slow pacing would cause viewers to switch off, but Lynch understood that, as long as we were infused with a sufficient sense of mystery, we'd be unable to.

Lynch gave his audience time to absorb the scene and to be affected by its soundtrack and atmosphere. When you are focused on the moment and fall into a state of mindfulness like this, the past and future cease to be relevant. The parts of the brain needed to model them become quieter. In broad-strokes neurological terms, the audience are processing the world in a style more strongly associated with the right hemisphere of the brain than the left. They are absorbing the changes occurring in the world rather than analysing and predicting them. They are thinking intuitively rather than intellectually.

Lynch, then, was leading his audience into a mental state unlike that generated by most movies. In that moment and in that state, what you feel about the unfolding scene is a genuine, unfiltered, uncensored reaction. It is not a simple echo of the emotion that the filmmaker has chosen for you. It is the difference between being told something and realising it for yourself, in a moment of revelation.

What Lynch did, then, was different to what the great

majority of filmmakers do. Most directors, essentially, force emotions onto you. They decide what they want you to feel and then push that feeling onto you through images that stimulate your mirror neurons. Lynch, in contrast, put you in a place where emotions would naturally rise out of you. These emotions would appear unexpectedly, and with little warning. They would also be genuine. The feelings that arise are how you feel about the scene, not what you are expected to feel about it.

An emotion felt in this way is not just an echo of something you are shown. It is a real expression of your psyche, and it reveals how deeply you are capable of feeling, especially about material that is dark and on the boundaries of your experience. Lynch had the ability to put the audience in a position where they actively encountered their own emotions, rather than passively observing predetermined feelings like a stream of tourists visiting a landmark. Importantly, Lynch was not prescribing exactly what it was that you should be feeling. He was secure enough in his belief that the ideas he loved would also generate reactions in others.

The audience's role in the impact of the film was something that Lynch always understood intuitively. As his long-term audio collaborator Dean Hurley explained, 'There is a school of thought that says movies in general do not actually happen on the screen, they happen inside the mind of the viewer. Which means that you are orchestrating these image and sound triggers in order for a viewer to complete the actual thing.' As Lynch wrote, 'I like the saying: "The world is as you are." And I think films are as you are. That's why, although the frames of a film are always the same – the same number, in the same sequence, with the same sounds – every screening is different.'

LYNCHIAN

Through meditation, David Lynch studied the mind and he studied attention. He understood the role it played in bringing the world into existence, just as he understood the role that the viewer's mind played in creating his films. This is why he would always insist that it was not his role to explain what his films meant. Instead, he would always insist that if people just watched the movie, they would have an experience – and that experience was everything they needed to know about the movie. He knew that his films didn't exist on the screen in the front of the cinema, they played out in minds sufficiently absorbed in what he was showing. This experience would be different for everyone, so he was in no position to explain what the film was about.

The definition of 'Lynchian' in the *Oxford English Dictionary* states that the word refers to something 'Characteristic, reminiscent, or imitative of the films or television work of David Lynch.' Exactly in what way a thing is characteristic of his films is not something the dictionary tries to define. In the face of this absence, it is often assumed that those important qualities consist of the visual, audio or narrative tropes Lynch developed over his career – but, as we've noted, the use of these by other filmmakers never feels truly Lynchian. It is when the state of mind that he put his audience into is included in that definition that we start to see what Lynchian means. Those who copy Lynch's end results, be they a young film student or a modern AI, never produce work that has the same impact. If they truly wanted to be Lynchian, they would need to copy his process instead, comfortable with the fact that the end results would be entirely different.

With his cigarettes, sincerity and striking hair, David Lynch played the role of a kooky cinematic auteur perfectly.

He was the singular genius and visionary behind those characters and those worlds. It made sense, in this context, that the definition of 'Lynchian' should be whatever David Lynch did. Yet what he was doing was leaving space for us in his work, then using all his skills to put us into a state of mind where we would tumble into that space. These skills were honed by a lifetime dedicated to the Art Life, above and beyond even his own relationships. All this work was needed to hone his talent to the point where he could successfully put us in a similar mental space to how he saw the world. In a sense all great films do this, of course, but it is often done accidentally. Every aspect of David Lynch's practice, in contrast, revolved around this relationship. He wanted to make us feel like he did when those ideas were first caught, in the depths of his mind. He wasn't trying to make us feel what his characters were feeling, he was trying to make us experience the world as he did. The meaning of the word 'Lynchian' may not be found in the dissection of his films but in the fact that we, the audience, are made Lynchian.

If we fall into his films often enough, we start to explore the world as David Lynch saw it. It is a place where the familiar, domestic, everyday world butts up against a great unknown that we can only experience as a fearful darkness. Mystery like this is seductive but terrifying, and that horror ultimately comes from our ignorance. The depth of this darkness makes the light of our known world shine brighter, but the terrifying things that are hidden within it don't always stay hidden. They can at times poke through and find us, motivated by impulses we will never understand. They appear to us in the form of mystery – a mystery so deep and fundamental that it threatens to tear up our sparse understanding of the world, leaving us changed for ever.

LYNCHIAN

As Lynch once said, 'We're not experiencing the ultimate reality: the "real" is hiding all through life, but we don't see it. We mistake it for all these other things. Fear is based on not seeing the whole thing and, if you could get there and see the whole thing, fear is out of the window.' This was the understanding that underpins all his films.

23

David Lynch's last high-profile project was an acting role. He appeared in the last scene of *The Fabelmans*, Steven Spielberg's semi-autobiographical coming of age movie. It was released in 2022. 'At first I didn't want to do it,' Lynch said. 'And the reason is, when it comes to acting, I've purposely tried to stay away from it, giving the likes of Harrison Ford and George Clooney a chance at their careers.' But Spielberg cannily enlisted his beloved Laura Dern to help persuade him, so he read the script and found that he liked the scene. Lynch agreed to do it on the proviso that he received a large bag of Cheetos in return.

The film was a lightly fictionalised retelling of the troubles in Spielberg's own parents' relationship, at the point when he was about to fulfil his childhood dream of becoming a filmmaker. The last scene, Spielberg has said, was an accurate re-creation of something that happened to him, as close as his memory could make it. This was the moment that the eager young wannabe filmmaker met one of the greatest directors of Hollywood's Golden Age.

At the end of the movie Sammy Fabelman, the character representing young Spielberg, is offered the chance to meet 'the greatest film director who ever lived'. This turned out to be the great John Ford, and Spielberg cast David Lynch to play him. From the moment Lynch walked into the film – marching slightly dazed into his office with an eye-patch and with lipstick marks around his face, his elderly assistant chasing after him with a box of tissues – it was as if Spielberg's film had slipped into one of Lynch's. This feeling was reinforced by the long, slow sequence which followed of Lynch as Ford lighting a cigar. Devoid of any narrative purpose other than to focus on fire, smoke and the sound of the cigar, this was filmed in the period after Lynch was diagnosed with emphysema, but before he gave up smoking.

Eventually Lynch's John Ford turns his attention to the young aspiring filmmaker in his office, and proceeds to lecture him not on filmmaking, but on art. Gruffly and aggressively, he explains the difference between images framed in a way that makes them interesting, and images which are 'boring as shit'. This re-created a moment in time in which a baton was passed, from John Ford's old Hollywood to Steven Spielberg's age of blockbusters and high-concept wonder.

It fell to David Lynch to pass on this lesson – to insist that we see images as art, and that filmmaking requires that those images are not just there to propel a story, but must have value and power in themselves. Spielberg's character then leaves the office and walks off into the sunset, and the camera reframes as instructed. The message is that Spielberg is now ready to remake Hollywood in his own image, having learnt the lesson of Ford and Lynch.

'Good luck to you, and get the fuck out of my office,' Lynch's Ford tells the young Spielberg, who mutters a 'thank you' before he leaves. This leads into the last shot of David Lynch, his final contribution to cinema. He removes the cigar from his mouth, smiles, and says, 'My pleasure.'

Then he was gone.

Silencio.

Notes and Sources

A book such as this is indebted to the four main sources of first-hand, in-depth biographical interviews with David Lynch. These are the books *Lynch on Lynch*, edited by Chris Rodley, *Room to Dream* by David Lynch and Kristine McKenna, *Catching the Big Fish* by David Lynch and the documentary *The Art Life*, directed by Olivia Neergaard-Holm, Rick Barnes and Jon Nguyen. All four are superb and highly recommended to all of Lynch's fans.

Chapter 1

'The outpouring of love': Naomi Watts, *Live with Kelly and Mark*, WABC-TV, 21 January 2025.
'There are certain figures': Richard Ayoade, *The Adam Buxton Podcast*, episode 242, 11 April 2025.

Chapter 2

'My father frequently experimented': *Lynch on Lynch*, ed. Chris Rodley, p. 10.
'We drive out of Boise': *Room to Dream*, David Lynch and Kristine McKenna, p. 20.
'Because I grew up in a perfect world': *Lynch on Lynch*, ed. Chris Rodley, p. 11.

NOTES AND SOURCES

'Night kind of magical': *Room to Dream*, David Lynch and Kristine McKenna, p. 26.

'I don't know what we were doing': *The Art Life* (2016), directed by Olivia Neergaard-Holm, Rick Barnes and Jon Nguyen.

'She sat down on the curb': *Room to Dream*, David Lynch and Kristine McKenna, p. 26.

Chapter 3

'Totally cool': *Lynch on Lynch*, ed. Chris Rodley, p. 13.

'There was something in the air': Ibid., pp. 4–5.

'Also despised all that goodness': *Room to Dream*, David Lynch and Kristine McKenna, p. 8.

'Lunch just appears': Ibid., p. 457.

'Would get so fired up': *IndieWire's Filmmaker Toolkit* podcast, 'The Sound Design of David Lynch with Studio Manager Dean Hurley', 10 July 2025.

'Thrilled my soul': *Lynch on Lynch*, ed. Chris Rodley, p. 9.

'*The Art Spirit* became the Art Life': *The Art Life* (2016), directed by Olivia Neergaard-Holm, Rick Barnes and Jon Nguyen.

Chapter 4

'For me, living the art life': *Catching the Big Fish*, David Lynch, p. 11.

'I had no doubt that he loved me': *Room to Dream*, David Lynch and Kristine McKenna, p. 69.

'Sat me down and said': Ibid., p. 111.

'David was the big love of my life': '"Es ist die Zeit, die Heilt"', by Herlinde Koelbl, *Die Zeit*, 14 February 2010.

'There's no malice in Dad': *Room to Dream*, David Lynch and Kristine McKenna, p. 183.

'I never was going to get married': *Lynch on Lynch*, ed. Chris Rodley, p. 80.

'After I had Lula, he disappeared': 'David Lynch: "You gotta be selfish. It's a terrible thing"', by Rory Carroll, *Guardian*, 23 June 2018.

'I need you to know': *Room to Dream*, David Lynch and Kristine McKenna, p. 452.

'You gotta be selfish': 'David Lynch: "You gotta be selfish. It's a terrible thing"', by Rory Carroll, *Guardian*, 23 June 2018.

'Is not good at close relationships': *Room to Dream*, David Lynch and Kristine McKenna, p. 452.

'When David looks at you': Ibid., pp. 480–1.

Chapter 5

'All my paintings are organic': *Lynch on Lynch*, ed. Chris Rodley, p. 22.

'Black has depth': Ibid., p. 20.

'A lot of my paintings come from memories': Ibid., p. 10.

'You learn pretty quickly': Ibid., p. 28.

'I learned that just beneath the surface': Ibid., p. 8.

'There was a thick, thick fear': *The Art Life* (2016), directed by Olivia Neergaard-Holm, Rick Barnes and Jon Nguyen.

'Philadelphia is my greatest influence': *David Lynch Teaches Creativity and Film*, Masterclass.com.

'Philadelphia [...] was so good for me': *The Art Life* (2016), directed by Olivia Neergaard-Holm, Rick Barnes and Jon Nguyen.

'What the average person sees': *Room to Dream*, David Lynch and Kristine McKenna, p. 152.

NOTES AND SOURCES

'One time I used some hair remover': *Lynch on Lynch*, ed. Chris Rodley, p. 23.

'I don't necessarily love rotting bodies': *Catching the Big Fish*, David Lynch, p. 121.

'Near the end of the visit': *The Art Life* (2016), directed by Olivia Neergaard-Holm, Rick Barnes and Jon Nguyen.

Chapter 6

'Movies didn't mean anything to me': *Room to Dream*, David Lynch and Kristine McKenna, p. 51.

'I wasn't taking drugs': *Catching the Big Fish*, David Lynch, p. 13.

'The core event of the David Lynch creation myth': *Room to Dream*, David Lynch and Kristine McKenna, p. 67.

'I remember David said something about': Mark Frost, 'Northwest Passage: Creating the Pilot' documentary, *Twin Peaks: The Entire Mystery*, Blu-ray box set, disk 8.

Chapter 8

'The ocean of pure consciousness': *Catching the Big Fish*, David Lynch, p. 47.

'It's absurd if a filmmaker needs to say': Ibid., p. 19.

'I felt *Eraserhead*, I didn't think it': *Room to Dream*, David Lynch and Kristine McKenna, p. 95.

'A bare room has a number of 2': *Lynch on Lynch*, ed. Chris Rodley, p. 23.

'This is for me a good-luck thing': *Film 90: Barry Norman's Cannes Diary*, BBC One, Wednesday, 23 May 1990.

'Suddenly a little wind-like thing': *Lynch on Lynch*, ed. Chris Rodley, p. 102.

'My eyes went up the pedestal': *Wild Card with Rachel Martin* podcast, 13 June 2024.

'Your soul has set you face to face': *Twin Peaks*, episode 16, 'Arbitrary Law', 1 December 1990.

Chapter 9

'David was a lot darker before': *Room to Dream*, David Lynch and Kristine McKenna, p. 105.

'It made her cry because': Ibid., p. 131.

'Before I started meditating': Ibid., p. 131.

'Someone arbitrarily says you got to': 'Impressions: A Journey Behind the scenes of Twin Peaks: A Pot of Boiling Oil', *Twin Peaks: The Return*, Blu-ray box set, disk 8.

'This is a fucking mess': 'Impressions: A Journey Behind the scenes of Twin Peaks: The Polish Accountant', *Twin Peaks: The Return*, Blu-ray box set, disk 8.

'This anger comes up in me': *Room to Dream*, David Lynch and Kristine McKenna, p. 166.

'David, you're a nicer guy than I am': 'An Introduction to David Lynch', *Twin Peaks: The Entire Mystery*, Blu-ray box set, disk 5.

'David needs a lot of care': *Room to Dream*, David Lynch and Kristine McKenna, p. 445.

Chapter 10

'I think I may have gone': *The Making of Star Wars: Return of the Jedi*, J.W. Rinzler, p. 42.

'Bizarre ... but interesting': Ibid., p. 207.

'Crawling into a phonebooth': 'David Lynch meets George Lucas', https://www.youtube.com/watch?v=EJQ4vCu-SoU.

'I thought, Okay, I'll go meet Dino': *Room to Dream*, David Lynch and Kristine McKenna, p. 192.

'I always admired George': 'David Lynch meets George Lucas', https://www.youtube.com/watch?v=EJQ4vCu-SoU.

Chapter 11

'I realized that the thing he remembers': *Room to Dream*, David Lynch and Kristine McKenna, p. 420.

'I do see a lot of myself in Jeffrey': Ibid., p. 207.

'The more darkness you can gather up': *Lynch on Lynch*, ed. Chris Rodley, p. 23.

Chapter 12

'It's twilight – with maybe a streetlight on': *Lynch on Lynch*, ed. Chris Rodley, p. 134.

'The idea is the whole thing': *Catching the Big Fish*, David Lynch, p. 83.

'It's weird, because when you veer off': Ibid., p. 83.

'I didn't have a script': Ibid., p. 145.

'If you appreciate slipping into another world': 'Back to Mulholland Drive' documentary, *Mulholland Drive*, Blu-ray.

'Waking dreams are the ones that are important': *Lynch on Lynch*, ed. Chris Rodley, p. 15.

Chapter 13

'We were out in the parking lot': *Lynch on Lynch*, ed. Chris Rodley, p. 165.

'I'd been auditioning for ten years': 'Naomi Watts, Laura

Dern & Patricia Arquette Tell David Lynch Stories', *W* magazine YouTube channel, 25 April 2017.

'**David Lynch is the most kind**': 'The Straight Story Making Of' documentary, *The Straight Story*, Blu-ray.

'**I think any actor who's worked with**': 'Moving Through Time: Fire Walk with Me Memories' documentary, *Twin Peaks: The Entire Mystery*, Blu-ray box set, disk 10.

'**If I ran my set with fear**': *Catching the Big Fish*, David Lynch, p. 73.

'**David said, "Russ, let's do it again"**': *Room to Dream*, David Lynch and Kristine McKenna, p. 254.

'**I remember, in the pilot**': 'Twin Peaks: How Laura Palmer's death marked the rebirth of TV drama', by Andrew Anthony, *Observer*, 21 March 2010.

'**Imagine being a child and seeing**': *Room to Dream*, David Lynch and Kristine McKenna, p. 337.

'***Wild at Heart* was such an intimate movie**': 'Naomi Watts, Laura Dern & Patricia Arquette Tell David Lynch Stories', *W* magazine YouTube channel, 25 April 2017.

'**I love you & I miss you**': Sherilyn Fenn on Instagram, @sherilyn_fennxo, 28 July 2025.

'**I loved him and will miss him**': Michael Horse on Instagram, @officialdeputyhawkk, 16 January 2025.

'**He was my north star**': Mädchen Amick on Instagram, @madchenamick, 16 January 2025.

'**I loved him so much**': Isabella Rossellini on Instagram, @isabellarossellini, 17 January 2025.

'**I will love and miss you**': Laura Dern on Instagram, @lauradern, 21 January 2025.

'**The true Willy Wonka of filmmaking**': 'Lara Flynn Boyle Remembers Her "Twin Peaks" Creator David Lynch: "There

Goes the True Willy Wonka of Filmmaking"', by Anthony D'Alessandro, *Deadline*, 16 January 2025.

Chapter 14

'Is at least 50 per cent of it': 'A Slice of Lynch' documentary, *Twin Peaks: The Entire Mystery*, Blu-ray box set, disk 3.
'As a member of the bureau': *Twin Peaks*, episode 16, 'Arbitrary Law', 1 December 1990.

Chapter 15

'Often there is something in the air': *Lynch on Lynch*, ed. Chris Rodley, p. 190.
'I just had, you know, a bad smell': Ibid., p. 121.
'First hearing it – total bullshit': *Wild Card with Rachel Martin* podcast, 13 June 2024.
'People capable of liking some': *Timequake*, Kurt Vonnegut, pp. 144–5.

Chapter 16

'Except now for Richard Pryor': *A Supposedly Fun Thing I'll Never Do Again*, David Foster Wallace, p. 189.
'Suddenly, if it's a Black man': *Lynch on Lynch*, ed. Chris Rodley, p. 152.
'Almost an evil, satanic plot': Ibid., p. 153.
'Despite the fact that the perpetration': Ibid., p. xii.
'It's nothing to do with right wing': Ibid., p. 205.
'He could go down as one of the greatest': 'David Lynch: "You gotta be selfish. It's a terrible thing"', by Rory Carroll, *Guardian*, 23 June 2018.

NOTES AND SOURCES

'**David Lynch could go down as**': 'Trump jokes David Lynch's career "is over" as he quotes Guardian interview', *Guardian News* YouTube channel, 26 June 2018.

'**I can tell you that after**': Jennifer Lynch (@thinkajen) in response to an 8 August 2025 TikTok post by @glitterbom. Details of the Roman Polanski petition signatures can be found at https://www.imdb.com/list/ls090808434.

'**I told them, those clown comics**': *Twin Peaks: The Return*, part 4, 21 May 2017.

Chapter 17

'**The devil took the form of fire.**': *Twin Peaks*, episode 5, 10 May 1990.

Chapter 18

'**The thing that kills me is**': 'A Slice of Lynch' documentary, *Twin Peaks: The Entire Mystery*, Blu-ray box set, disk 3.

'**I've seen the movie twenty-six times**': 'Back to Mulholland Drive' documentary, *Mulholland Drive*, Blu-ray.

'**Mystery is good, confusion is bad**': *Lynch on Lynch*, ed. Chris Rodley, p. 227.

'**Clues are beautiful things**': Ibid., p. 287.

Chapter 19

'**I walked out at 1:30 a.m.**': Mark Frost interviewed by Samira Ahmed, *Front Row*, BBC Radio 4, 9 June 2025.

NOTES AND SOURCES

Chapter 20

'David was a vegetarian then': *Room to Dream*, David Lynch and Kristine McKenna, p. 179.

'I'm heavily into sugar': *Lynch on Lynch*, ed. Chris Rodley, p. 90.

'I can hardly walk across a room': 'David Lynch Started Smoking at Age 8 — Now He Needs Oxygen to Walk: "It's a Big Price to Pay"', by Eileen Finan, *People*, 14 November 2024.

'Yes, I have emphysema': David Lynch on X, @DAVID_LYNCH, 5 August 2024.

'I loved the smell of tobacco': 'David Lynch Started Smoking at Age 8 — Now He Needs Oxygen to Walk: "It's a Big Price to Pay"', by Eileen Finan, *People*, 14 November 2024.

Chapter 21

'He got sick several times': *Room to Dream*, David Lynch and Kristine McKenna, p. 487.

'At one point he said to me': Ibid., p. 488.

Chapter 22

'There is a school of thought': *IndieWire's Filmmaker Toolkit* podcast, 'The Sound Design of David Lynch with Studio Manager Dean Hurley', 10 July 2025.

'I like the saying': *Catching the Big Fish*, David Lynch, p. 21.

'We're not experiencing the ultimate reality': *Lynch on Lynch*, ed. Chris Rodley, pp. 243–4.

Chapter 23

'**At first I didn't want to do it**': 'David Lynch Requested a Bag of Cheetos to Appear in Steven Spielberg's "The Fabelmans": "Any Chance I Can, I Get Them"', by Armando Tinoco, *Deadline*, 19 December 2023.

Acknowledgements

This book exists thanks to the heroic efforts of my publisher and editor Jenny Lord, who somehow bypassed the strange and arcane timelines of publishing in order to pay timely tribute to David Lynch. Thanks also to all at Weidenfeld & Nicolson, including Lily McIlwain, Harry Taylor, Tom Noble and Georgia Goodall. Thanks to Steve Marking for the cover and to Paul Stark, Millie Gee and Rhys Timson for the audio version. Thanks also to my agent Sarah Ballard and Liv Bignold at C&W.

And, as always, all love to Joanne, Lia and Isaac.